THE PIEDMONT GARDEN

The Piedmont Garden

HOW TO GROW BY THE CALENDAR, Second Edition

by

Juanita Bartlett Garrison

Illustrations by

Carl Edward Gross

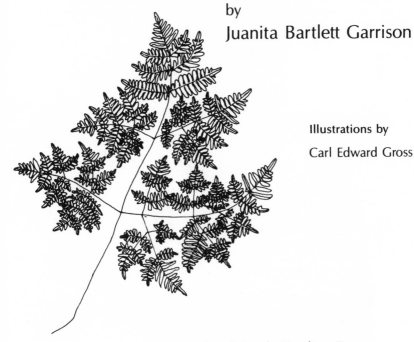

University of South Carolina Press

Copyright © University of South Carolina 1981, 1990

Second Edition
Published in Columbia, South Carolina, by the
University of South Carolina Press

Manufactured in the United States of America

00 99 98 97   5 4 3 2

Library of Congress Cataloging in Publication Data

Garrison, Juanita Bartlett.
    The Piedmont garden : how to grow by the calendar / by Juanita
  Bartlett Garrison ; illustrations by Carl Edward Gross.—2nd ed.
        p.   cm.
    Includes index.
    ISBN 0-87249-717-8
    1. Gardening—Piedmont (U.S. : Region)   I. Title.
SB453.2.P54G37   1990
635.9'0975—dc20   90-39323

Lovingly dedicated to our younger son,

James Bartlett "Bart" Garrison
July 19, 1960–May 9, 1990

Who died in a silo accident at Denver Downs Farm
while this second edition was in its
last phases of publication

CONTENTS

CONTENTS

PREFACE

Welcome to the second edition of *The Piedmont Garden: How to Grow by the Calendar*. Some of the material has been enlarged and revised to include newer varieties and information on new products and garden practices. It has additional chapters on vegetable gardening and a listing of plant societies.

Most of the material in this book has appeared in more or less the same form as weekly and monthly newspaper columns.

Although the botanical information is correct, *The Piedmont Garden* is not a scholarly horticultural treatise for the experienced gardener. It is for the beginning gardener who knows little but wants to learn. I hope this material will help him to start and to continue his delightful journey as a gardener and give him a little smile as he goes about his tasks.

Even as a youngster I loved growing flowers. I can remember scratching a hole in the ground, putting in marigold seeds bought at school, and later wondering why they didn't grow.

Poor things. They were planted in dry, hardpan soil and never had a chance. As a compensation for increasing my waistline and decreasing my eyesight, the years have brought a little more knowledge about what is one of the loveliest of all avocations: the tending of a garden.

J. B. G.
Denver Downs Farm
Anderson, S.C.
1990

January

First Week
Resolutions and Such

By now you have lived with and broken the resolutions made with such eagerness and determination a few days ago for your general improvement. So, now that those are out of the way, perhaps we could suggest a few just for gardeners.

These came to me Saturday when I had my little unpaid crew cleaning yards. Daughter Gaye raked leaves, and because her nearby transistor made noises somewhat like sounds you would expect from a wartime field hospital, I was for once thankful for the noise of the shredder that our oldest son Tom and I were operating.

Not wishing to be presumptuous, I offer only nine gardening commandments.

FIRST, be careful how you interpret the descriptions in garden catalogs. When something is listed as "easy to grow," it doesn't mean you can poke a hole in hardpan soil, drop in a seed, forget the poor thing, and expect it to produce flower-show-quality blooms in a few weeks.

The description means comparatively. You don't have to have humidifiers, underground water systems, and all manner of things, for instance, to grow a marigold, but you do have to give it some care.

SECOND, plan where you are going to put things before you order them lest a passing neighbor find you standing in the middle of your yard with glazed eyes, three packs of scabiosa seed in your hand, and mumbling to yourself.

This planning will save you effort, money, and time, three commodities I have always prized rather highly. It's easier to plan these things at your leisure some evening when everyone else is watching The Box than on that beautiful day when you are trying to get a dozen garden chores done at one time.

THIRD, don't bite off more than you can chew. Decide at what time and for how long each day you will work in your garden. For some, early morning is satisfactory; then she can go inside and tidy both herself and her house for the day. Others prefer late afternoon, but if you have a son in Little League, don't count on this hour. If you have a full-time job, your time is even more limited.

I contend that it is far better to have a properly done small bed or edging around the house than to have a yard filled with neglected plants and shrubs.

Plan two or three periods of yard work each week, just as you plan a trip to the grocery store, changing bed linen, or other routine tasks.

FOURTH, keep tools in their proper place. Few things are as exasperating as having to look for a tool when you want it. Get your tools in good order, determine a permanent storage place for them, and keep them there even if you have to threaten to make heads roll. Always put them back even if you are going to return to the same task later in the day.

FIFTH, try something new. Garden catalogs list thousands of kinds of seeds. Not even the seed company grows all of them in one place and neither can you; but with all those to choose from, don't limit yourself to the Big Three: marigolds, petunias, and zinnias. Everybody has her favorites but each year try one or two new flowers or shrubs. You may find something you really like.

SIXTH, make at least one permanent improvement in your yard each year. It may be an elaborate effort such as a patio, driveway, greenhouse, or fence, or a much smaller one, such as a new specimen shrub or tree, or a garden bench, or shooting the neighbor's dog.

SEVENTH, become a specialist. I don't mean specialize to the point that you will write scholarly papers and make public addresses, but select a plant that has always appealed to you and learn all you can about it. Learn its botanical as well as its common name; learn its history; try the different varieties; learn to hybridize. This can be your own little world of expertise—and think how clever you will sound at parties.

EIGHTH, plan, plant, and pamper one flower to enter a show, whether it is a garden-club show or the open shows at the county fair. Even if you don't win, you will learn a lot about the flower.

NINTH, and most important, enjoy your gardening.

Second Week
CAMELLIAS

Camellias are beginning to bloom. The sasanquas have either finished or been finished by the cold, but *Camellia japonicas* are just coming into their own loveliness and will continue until late February and March.

Mrs. R. F. Brownlee of our town is one of the Piedmont's most successful growers of camellias and is also a camellia show judge. She and her late husband first became interested in camellias many years ago when they bought some for foundation plants. Like many other growers they soon became enamored with the shrub because of its delightful habit of blooming in winter when the rest of the garden is asleep. Over the years they became specialists growing, grafting, showing, and sharing their camellias. Mrs. Brownlee was quite willing to share her practices with other gardeners who want to grow the camellia, traditionally a southern shrub although some varieties will do well in the North.

Camellias require partial shade and will not do well in either full shade or full sun. They should also be protected from strong winds. Most growers meet these conditions by planting them among pines. They are also demanding about their soil, but I suppose anything as beautiful as a camellia can be forgiven some peculiarities. They won't do at all in clay. They need acid soil rich in humus.

To plant a new shrub, Mrs. Brownlee digs a large hole 2 or 3 feet wide and fills it with good soil, composted manure, and decayed leaves. Another thing the plant requires is good drainage, so if your site doesn't drain too well, the problem can be corrected at planting time by making the hole a foot deeper than necessary and filling the extra depth with sand and good soil.

Immediately after the plants are in the ground, water them thoroughly and mulch. Camellias have a growing spurt in spring and another in late summer, so don't move the plant during or between these times. This leaves early spring and fall as moving times. Late fall is the better because the plant can get established over the winter to take the onslaught of our hot summers.

New plants should be mulched immediately. Mrs. Brownlee saves all fallen leaves for mulching established plants in the spring, putting the leaves right on top of the old mulch and then covering them with pine needles. The mulch helps keep the plants warm in winter, cool in summer, damp during dry periods, and weed-free most of the time. As the old mulch decays it builds up the soil with more acid humus.

She also follows a fertilizing program in the spring, beginning when the plants are still in bloom. Mrs. Brownlee makes three light feedings about three weeks apart using a commercial camellia fertilizer. For your own camellias, use a scant ½ cup for very large plants and about half that or less for the smaller ones, depending on the plant's size. Pull back the mulch and sprinkle it on top of the ground. Don't work it into the soil because camellias, like most shade-growing plants, have shallow root systems that can be damaged easily by digging.

Even strong, healthy plants like Mrs. Brownlee's are attacked by insects. In spring she uses a commercial spray formulated for camellias and citrus plants. Mrs. Brownlee warns that the undersides of the leaves must be sprayed.

6

They also have a problem with "die-back," the cause of which is unknown. When the end of a limb dies, the only thing to do is to cut it off and burn it.

Camellias don't resent pruning and can take it almost any time of the year if you are sure to cut back to a growth bud, otherwise, the stem left beyond it will die. Any severe pruning to encourage bushy growth or to reduce the tree's size should be done in spring right after blooming before new growth starts so the plant will be in leaf again by summer.

One reason many growers are disappointed in their plants is because they select varieties inappropriate for their locality. Prospective growers should check with nurseries in their own areas and select those plants which grow best there.

Another camellia-growing friend who knows much more than I do recommends the following hybrid varieties which will do well in the colder areas of the Piedmont: Dr. Clifford Parks (red), Dr. Louis Pollizzi (white-orchid pink), E. G. Waterhouse (light pink double), El Dorado (light pink), Fire Chief (red semi-double), Glenn's Orbit (deep orchid pink semi-double).

You may disbud camellias as soon as you can determine the difference between a growth bud and a flower bud. You can disbud by simply breaking off the unwanted buds so the remaining ones will make larger flowers, but a more careful way is to stick a large needle or hat pin through the bud from the tip end down to the stem. This lets air inside and the bud will soon fall off. This technique allows you to avoid accidentally removing buds which you want to remain on the bush.

Gibbing is another camellia practice. This is a slang word for applying gibberellic acid according to package directions to the flower buds in August or September to get earlier and larger blooms. This is especially useful if you have a variety that doesn't take the cold too well. By gibbing you get the bloom before the freeze does. The most spectacular blooms come from those plants that are both disbudded and gibbed.

Camellias are propagated by (1) taking hardwood cuttings in July and August and inserting them in damp sand, (2) grafting a scion from the desired plant onto seedling stock in late spring, and (3) by sowing seeds. The last is the least satisfactory because it takes about five to seven years from seed to bloom and the blooms, usually single, are rarely true to the parent.

Third Week
BERMUDA GRASS

If you are a parent of school-age children, you quickly notice when they are home because of snow. The first indication last week was the 37 glasses in the sink, and the second indication was that at any given time between 7:00 and 11:50 A.M. someone was eating breakfast. It was a diverting experience and we established certain facts that might be of interest to students of human behavior, to wit:

That it is possible for an American youth to eat 18 hours a day for five days without incurring any permanent injury to the digestive system;

That a used harrow disk makes a better sled than a sled;

That a Monopoly game can last 120 hours without a winner;

That the survival of the 12 to 18 age group is dependent upon the telephone; and

That after a while, even children tire of television, telephones, video games and tapes and are ready to return to school.

During all the mopping of water from dripping boots, searching for misplaced gloves, and trying to identify the owners of certain unfamiliar articles of clothing, there came a nice note from Ellen Franklin asking, with a forward look to spring, how to rid her vegetable garden of Bermuda grass. For years I have fought Bermuda tooth and nail in my flower beds while at the same time my Ed was putting the stuff, deliberately, mind you, in his pastures. All of which proves that a thing can be good or bad, depending on how it's used. I have threatened to come back and haunt him if he lets Bermuda grow over my grave.

Bermuda has tenacious qualities that make it a good erosion fighter on banks, waterways, and such, and it is highly desirable for a permanent pasture because cattle like its taste, and it is high in protein, calcium, and phosphoric acid. But when it is encircling your irises, roses, strawberries or green beans, you have to summon all your Christian charity to find something good to say about it.

There are three ways you can meet the invasion of Bermuda grass into your vegetables and flowers: prayer, concrete, and unconditional surrender.

If you are unfamiliar with the first, dissatisfied with the second, and too proud for the third, you might consider alternatives one and two as suggested by my former local county agent Herb Marrett.

Alternative one is to abandon your garden spot for a period. If the area is small you can use a gas on it which kills all grass seeds and plants. This requires careful doing because the edges of the plastic covering the area must be tightly sealed. Follow the instructions on the gas which is available at most garden centers. There are also several herbicides which you can spray over the entire garden. After the recommended time you can till and rake the area removing all the dead plant material.

If you don't follow the time schedule and plant too soon, the seeds won't germinate and any plants you set out won't live.

I really don't care for the herbicides because you have to be very careful in applying them but mostly because the soil is filled with all kinds of little live things and when you start killing weeds and grasses you get these also.

Alternative two is to cultivate. This is what I do. There is one bed that has to be completely cleared each spring.

Bermuda grass, *Cynodon dactylon,* is called wire grass in some parts of the country and devil grass in others. It comes at you both ways by sending out runners on top of the ground and by shooting out rhizomes underneath the soil to send up a plant several inches from the mother plant.

Hand pulling Bermuda would be impossible for a large vegetable plot. Instead, in the early spring, run your tiller or whatever cultivator you use over the plot, then with a garden rake and grubbing hoe go over the whole area removing the Bermuda roots. In about a week, when both your back and disposition have improved, do the whole thing again and you should have out most of the roots.

After your vegetables come up, cultivate around them with a hoe to get any shoots that appear. You can also hand pull any sprigs you see.

After you've done all this, a good deterrent to further growth, although certainly not foolproof, is to put down a thick mulch.

Put black plastic between the rows, or, if this is too much trouble or expense, lay about three or four thicknesses of newspaper and top with leaves, hay, pine needles, grass clippings, or any other mulching material you have.

This mulch does two things. First, it keeps out light, which all plants, including even the plagued Bermuda, must have to live, and second, it keeps out most of the air, another requirement for plants.

A third advantage of this mulching is that after a summer, fall, and winter in the garden, the newspaper-leaf combination can be plowed into the soil next spring, further improving the site's organic contents.

About the same procedure can be followed among shrubs and flowers. Cultivate and rake to remove the roots, pull out new sprigs, and mulch. Bermuda is a special nuisance among perennials because you don't want to disturb their roots while trying to get out the Bermuda.

During the last several years our friends in the agricultural chemical business have come to the aid of the home gardener in the great Bermuda-grass war. Two of the most often-used products are Round Up and Poast, both contact sprays. This means that nearby plants must be protected from the drifting spray. The herbicides are sprayed directly onto the unwanted plants then in due time the plants die and can be dug. What happens in this: the leaves absorb the chemical sending it down into the roots which it kills. It will not affect the roots of other shrubs or plants if their foliage has not been sprayed.

Bermuda grass is a nuisance—one of the little problems that a gardener has to face and either accept or fight.

If it's any comfort, I've heard that nut grass and old age are both worse.

Fourth Week
CHRISTMAS CACTI

If this time last month you were enjoying your neighbor's Christmas cactus, now is the time to get yourself busy so you can have one just as pretty, or more so, by next Christmas.

This doesn't mean you have to carry on over the plant for a solid year; it will just give it plenty of growing time. The Christmas cactus, *Zygocactus truncatus,* is easily rooted and easily grown, therefore a good houseplant choice for the beginning gardener.

In talking about this beautiful plant with its chainlike flat limbs and its panicles of vibrant, rosy pink blooms I consulted two successful cactus growers: Mrs. Irene Stewart, North Second Street, Seneca, S.C., and the wife of our former pastor, Mrs. F. M. Lindler.

Mrs. Lindler has a green thumb, if you believe in such, all the way to her elbow and grows the most beautiful flowers, seemingly with ease but actually with much work and care.

Mrs. Stewart told me a most remarkable thing. She said she has a very large cactus in a peck bucket that has been in the same bucket, never repotted, for more than 30 years. You would think the poor thing would be so root-bound it couldn't breathe, but it was loaded with blooms this past Christmas as it has been every Christmas for 30 years.

Both Mrs. Stewart and Mrs. Lindler agree that the plant is easily rooted from a cutting of a couple of inches up to a large limb that is accidentally broken. It can be rooted in sand and transplanted or rooted directly in its permanent pot.

Mrs. Stewart does the latter, but Mrs. Lindler says she does better by rooting in sand, then moving the new little plant with a spoonful of sand still around the tender root into the permanent container.

They also agree the soil should be loose. After 30 years Mrs. Stewart admits she has forgotten what kind of soil is in her bucket, but it must have been pretty good stuff. She puts new plants into humusy soil. Mrs. Lindler says she uses a mixture of humus, garden soil, and sand to keep the soil porous.

A good soil recipe for most any flowering houseplant is 2 parts soil, 1 part peat, leaf mold or compost, and ½ part or 1 part sand. You can also add ½ tablespoon of bone meal and the same amount of lime for an average-size pot.

The new plants should be watered along, but don't keep them really damp. When they get to growing well, ease up on the watering and water them only when dry to the touch; too much water will cause the fleshy limbs to rot.

Mrs. Stewart says she feeds hers occasionally with a commercial houseplant food according to the box directions, and Mrs. Lindler waters her plant all summer with liquid manure to assure a hardy plant before carrying it inside in the fall.

12

While outdoors in the spring, summer, and autumn, the Christmas cactus should receive no more than a half day's sun; Mrs. Stewart's gets afternoon sun.

After it has been growing all summer, bring the plant inside about the middle of September or October and put it in a dark place. This doesn't mean a closet, but away from the direct sun, and stop watering for about a month to slow down the growth.

About the first of November, put it in a window with direct sun or a very bright window and resume watering. It should then start putting out buds and bloom by Christmas.

Mrs. Lindler says the only insect problem she has with her plants is the mealy bug, which appears as a little ball of cotton at the corners of leaves and stems. Using a window-cleaner spray bottle she sprays them with equal parts of rubbing alcohol and water, which she says works just as well as a commercial spray. The water also helps keep the plant clean and the alcohol may help keep it happy.

After its blooming period, the cactus should be allowed to rest awhile, although I don't really know what else you could make it do, but anyway, in the late winter or early spring every two or three years you should repot it into a slightly larger pot—everybody except Mrs. Stewart, that is.

Because most houseplants do better when they are slightly pot-bound, no great harm will be done if you are a year or two behind.

Instead of Christmas cactus, sometimes the plant is called Thanksgiving cactus because it often blooms in November. Following this line of thinking, those blooming in February could probably be called Valentine cacti.

If you want one that blooms at Christmas time, the best thing to do is to get a stem from someone whose plant already has its blooming calendar set for December. The November bloomers could probably be delayed until Christmas if their growth were slowed as we said above.

Fourth Week
TOMATOES

A survey taken by someone, not me because I was cleaning the hall closet that day, showed that 92 percent of all home gardeners grow tomatoes. I would have thought the percentage even higher than that because almost everyone who grows any vegetables at all has a few tomato plants.

You don't need a lot of tomatoes unless you are planning to can or make juice. A few well-tended plants will supply a family with enough tomatoes for eating and sharing all summer long.

You can wait until after frost and buy the plants but it's more fun to grow your own. Tomato plants started from seeds should be ready to transplant into the garden in about seven weeks. Determine your first frost-free date then count backward. For most of the Piedmont that means sowing seeds in mid-February.

Before that time though you must settle the selection of seeds. To do that you have to know how many plants you will need and where you are going to put them. Most vegetables are grown in a vegetable plot but tomatoes, especially for people who don't grow other vegetables, are sometimes set in flower borders, tucked away in a sunny corner of the yard, or grown in containers.

You may see on your seed packet an "I" or a "D." The "D" means the plant is a determinate or bush-type tomato that stops growing when it reaches a certain height and that all the tomatoes are likely to ripen about the same time or over a short period. This is the kind you want if you are canning or making juice.

If your package has an "I" it means the variety is indeterminate or a staking or caging tomato and that it will continue to grow and put out new blooms and fruit until frost.

There are dozens of varieties of tomatoes so the selection

will be a challenge. You will probably want to buy a hybrid variety. This means you get a more vigorous plant than the non-hybrid and one that is more disease resistant. The package will possibly be stamped with the letters VFN. The "VF" part means the variety is resistant to two major wilt diseases of tomatoes, verticillium and fusarium. The "N" refers to its resistance to nematodes. If the package also has a "T" that means it has tolerance for tobacco mosaic. Tomatoes attract about as many insects and diseases as roses so try to buy the resistant varieties.

Most seed packets do not tell you how many seeds are included but you can pretty well count on there not being many. You may want to plant a packet of the determinate and one of an indeterminate variety but if you need tomatoes only for eating then one packet of an indeterminate variety will be enough.

Start your seeds in a sterile medium using perlite, vermiculite, or purchased potting soil. These do not contain any nutrients for the young plants; the seedling subsists for a short time on the nourishment of the seed. Sow the seeds about ¼ inch deep, water well, and keep the seed flat in a light place such as a heated porch, window, or greenhouse. The seeds germinate best at 70°.

After the seedlings appear give them a few days then transplant, spacing them about 3 inches apart in deep containers such as clay flowerpots. When moving the seedlings lift them with small tool. The end of a paring knife or nail file will do. Hold them gently by the leaves; never squeeze the stem. When transplanted, water them well and give them plenty of light. After about a week begin giving them weekly feedings of a weak fertilizer solution.

When the plants are about six weeks old begin hardening them by putting them outdoors in the daytime and bringing them indoors at night. After three or four days of this leave them outside at night if the nights are frost free. After three days or more move the plants to their permanent location. Into the planting hole for each plant put a cup of lime and a generous portion of well-rotted manure, about a shovel full. Mix this all together and set the plant deeply, all the way to its first set of leaves. The tomato will send out roots all along the planted stem to make a strong plant.

Maturity dates vary with the variety but the time given is usually from transplanting not from seed sowing.

The site you select for tomatoes is very important. They need good drainage and good air circulation. If you have an area in your yard where water stands after a rain, don't put tomatoes there. Even with the addition of the lime and manure a soil which is mostly clay may not produce satisfactory tomatoes. You may need to add sand or peat to the row to loosen the soil. Don't plant tomatoes in an inside corner or any other place where the good air circulation is hampered. They need plenty of sun. If the only place you have for a few tomato plants is in a semi-shaded flower bed go ahead and put them there. The fruit will be small and the production light but if you neither want nor need many tomatoes this may be all right.

The determinate tomatoes which are usually bushy sprawling plants don't have to be actually staked but should have a heavy mulch to keep the tomatoes clean and to avoid decay that comes when they lie on the ground. The indeterminate plants must be staked or grown in cages or on a trellis. Put a 6- or 7-foot stake beside the transplant. Drive the stake into the ground enough to give it stability. As the plant grows "prune" it so that you have two strong limbs and tie these to the stake. You will have to continue tying as the plant grows.

Tomatoes have to have water. Use whatever method you prefer but they need moisture.

Notes for January

February

First Week
SEED CATALOGS

Next July when you have little pains that start at the nape of your neck and shoot out quick sparks to your shoulder and lower back, you will think you were temporarily insane when you planted all those seeds. But that is a long way off and right now the house is warm, you've had a good supper, things are fairly settled down for the evening, and you can begin one of the secret joys of a gardener's life: the perusal of the seed catalogs.

Now the fellow who neither cares about nor knows the difference between a sweet pea and a petunia will think you are a bit daft to see you flipping back and forth among the pages comparing soil requirements, periods of bloom, exposures, drought resistance, and other such stuff, but we shall think no more of him. This is our own little world where we dream of the loveliness we shall produce around home and farm this summer causing great envy among our friends and, more deliciously, among our enemies.

The catalogs arrive about the same time the little fellow with the diaper runs around hollering the New Year has come, as if eight straight hours of football were not signal enough. And they are beautiful things, these seed and nursery catalogs, with their colorful close-ups and enticing words.

Now let it be known that the seed business people are no dumb bunnies. Who else could get someone to pay $227,480 a pound for petunia seeds assuming you ever had to buy that much. (There are 252,000 petunia seeds per ounce. A current catalog offers one variety at $2.55 for 45 seeds.) Those beautiful pictures do exactly what they were planned for: get you to buy seed. Even if you do buy more than you plant many of them will keep in the fridge for several seasons, and think how much fun you had looking at the catalogs and making the selections.

21

If you don't get seed catalogs, it is your own fault. Pick up a garden magazine at the newsstand and you'll find dozens of ads for them. Although some companies do charge, most of the catalogs are free.

After your first excitement subsides, do some serious thinking about your yard. Don't plant just anything. We all know Rome wasn't built in a day, and neither were its gardens.

If you are moving into a new house with a bare yard, please make a plan either with a landscaper or a nurseryman, or use one of your own design after reading books and magazines about gardening.

The best way to do this is to steal a sheet of graph paper from your junior high schooler, or if you are interested in more detail, get a big 20 x 20 sheet from the bookstore. Draw the house to scale and put in driveways, etc.—about ¼ inch to equal a foot is a good scale to work with. Then take your list of shrubs and sketch them in considering their maximum growth. Number the shrubs and put a key down in the corner showing what each number stands for. Include trees, shrubs, flowers, and work areas.

If you like details and are finicky about the way you do things, draw little blobs for the shrubs and trees and fill them in solidly with your pencil as you plant each one. It gives you the same satisfaction as checking off a list.

The first planting season in a new house should be used for the lawn to prevent erosion. Projects two and three should be trees and foundation planting. If you really want flowers, scatter a few marigold seed about, but don't try to make any permanent beds this first year. If you get the lawn, trees, and foundation this first year, you should feel rather proud of yourself.

It's all very well to want a rose garden, a lily pond, an herb garden, a perennial border, and other such good things, but use a little sense and don't try to do it all at once.

The seed catalogs can be invaluable in planning your landscape. Suppose a garden book suggests a Russian olive and you have no more idea than a jay bird what one looks like. The nursery catalog will describe it for you, give its growth requirements, possibly provide a picture, and even offer it for sale.

Some catalogs offer basic foundation planting packages already worked out for you. These are usually pretty good, but you must check to be sure the suggested plants will do well in your area.

A helpful service some of the large seed companies are providing is to give little landscape plans for various areas in the garden. They show a diagram, give a color drawing or photograph of the planting's appearance when in bloom, and give a list of plant varieties. Some of these are offered as "packages" to purchase.

After you plan, you may be able to find some of the plants at your local nursery or in cans from the garden store. Shrubs from catalogs usually come with bare roots in a plastic bag with some kind of damp packing material around them. Get these into the ground as soon as possible. Therefore, know where you are going to use a plant before you buy it and get the soil ready before or while waiting for it to come.

Most catalogs throw little rewards at you for ordering early in the form of cash savings or bonus seeds and plants. Either way, you get the prize. If you get busy now and order seeds and shrubs early, you'll have nothing to do until they come except worry about the work.

Second Week
COMPOST HEAPS

I was first introduced to compost by a charming little woman who lived in the Richland community of Oconee County, S.C., some twenty years ago. To garden clubs she made a talk entitled "A Sense of Humus" in which she gave the members a thorough verbal thrashing for throwing away such good stuff as grapefruit rinds, eggs shells, and potato peelings.

That appealed to my stingy nature and my love affair with humus has continued over these years to the point that I think anyone who throws away organic matter that will decay and build better soil for your garden is almost un-Christian, un-American, and certainly unpatriotic.

To some the word compost is synonymous with animal waste. We won't pay any more attention to them; they're probably the same fellows who don't like to read seed catalogs. We know that compost, as referring to gardening, is that marvelous dark, rich, crumbly mixture for renovating soil that results from the mixing and decaying of several organic materials in a compost heap.

So if you haven't started your compost heap yet, there is still time to do so, and you'll have about three or four months for it to decompose before you need it.

To make a proper heap, according to Sir Albert Howard, the British agronomist usually considered the father of the organic method, you need two things. The first is the proper organic materials, and the second is the proper conditions to cause them to decompose. The ratio of plant matter to manure and soil is about 3 to 1 for the best humus.

Now you would think that living on a farm as I do there would be plenty of decayed matter for my petunia bed but this is not the case. The manure must be well rotted and composted and it is really better as a soil additive and builder when it is mixed with other materials in a compost heap. Therefore it is to my advantage and that of my petunia bed to make a compost heap. The advantage of farm living is that we have available materials to go into the heap.

The basis of most humus heaps is leaves. If you have a shredder, so much the better, or you can do a fair job by piling the leaves and running the lawn mower back and forth over them.

Other ingredients may be grass clippings, ground corn cobs, phosphate rock, cottonseed meal, coffee grounds, kitchen trimmings, sawdust, seaweed, wood ashes, manure, spoiled hay or straw, granite dust, or most any available plant material that will decay. Your pile should have some type of animal manure and soil.

Now you put your materials together, layer on layer like a sandwich, cover it all with soil, then wet it good and cover with plastic. You have to keep it moist and you should go out and turn it every couple of weeks so the decay will be hastened.

Now I admit this turning is hard work but if you will keep your compost heap a reasonable size the job won't be so threatening. A current garden catalog offers a compost tool. It consists of a handle like a hoe with prongs somewhat like a toggle bolt. They push up when you plunge the handle into the heap and fan out to lift and move the material when you pull it out. I haven't tried this, loyal to my pitchfork as I am, but it should work.

There are as many ways to make a compost pile as there are to make corn bread and every fellow thinks his way is best. Although the size and materials may vary this is one way to do it. Much depends on what materials are available. My late neighbor Harold Morehead, an excellent gardener, used no animal manure but always added some of the previous year's composted material because it contained the necessary bacteria to start the decomposition process.

You will use this marvelous humus in your flower beds and vegetable garden. Compost is not a fertilizer in the sense that you put it on this year and have to do so again next year. It is a soil rebuilder. Of course, better results are obtained if you do add some every year, but it doesn't go away in one growing season like fertilizer.

Once you've made a compost pile, your whole personality will change. You will become grasping in your efforts to secure things for it. You will look with covetous eyes on piles of gin trash, wood chips, peanut hulls, or any other decayable matter. You will pounce like an enraged Mother Nature upon a guest or maid who casually throws lettuce leaves or coffee grounds into the garbage. A child who throws away these kitchen treasures is taking his life in his hands. You will lie awake nights should the tea leaves go elsewhere but into your precious compost pile.

My neighbor Earle Mimms is an earnest organic gardener. He keeps a "getting ready" heap going all year. Into it he puts all the kitchen waste, ashes, grass clippings, and other decayable matter all during the year, and every now and then he throws a few shovelfuls of soil on top of it. In the fall he rakes and shreds leaves, then, sometime in January, he starts mixing his shredded leaves, some manure he has had lying in a pile, and the assorted material he has accumulated in his "getting ready" pile. He wets it down, covers it, and leaves it alone. It doesn't have to be turned as often if the material is shredded.

Even if you can't make a proper compost heap this year, you can start with a tiny one by marking a spot on the edge of your garden where you can put all the kitchen clippings and shovel some soil over it every now and then. In time this will decay to provide material for a small flower bed. Your project will be easier if you keep a container on your kitchen counter for this biodegradable material rather than throwing it in with the other garbage. In my kitchen a covered aluminum 2-quart "compost" pot occupies a permanent spot beside the sink. While you are considering garbage begin the practice of separating aluminum foil and cans, glass, and plastic soft-drink bottles to recycle.

Some gardeners make bins of wood with raised floors to permit air circulation, others make concrete block walls with an open end, some use bales of hay, and there are those who simply pile the stuff on the ground. I'm a ground piler myself.

If you are really serious about the project, carry some of the finished compost to your county agent's office, and he will have a soil sample made for you to discover if you need to add other ingredients to have properly balanced humus.

By our very nature we Farmers' Wives are thrifty. We like this economical and ecological way of improving our own small corners. If we aren't making the world a whole lot better, we have the pleasure of knowing we are in our own little way keeping it from getting any worse.

Third Week
TERRARIUMS

Anthropologists could call America a nation of fad followers. We always have some craze to keep us excited. Usually it is an established practice or custom that is suddenly "discovered" and sweeps the country. We have survived furniture repairing, Japanese flower arranging, patchwork, jogging, and for a time not too long ago it was terrariums which we also survived. Some people still make them and I'm glad because it is a charming indoor garden practice.

Terrariums have been with us a long time, going back to the period of the Edwardian box, a large glass enclosure for flowers and foliage plants. Our smaller houses of today require smaller "boxes" in the form of tabletop terrariums.

During the height of the terrarium craze I swam with three other women in torrents of rain down to Callaway Gardens in Georgia to attend a seminar on indoor gardening. The thing I learned most was how dumb I am. After seeing their magnificent greenhouses and recognizing only one plant in five, I was more than ever convinced that the world is filled with things I shall never know.

The terrarium program was conducted by a pretty and delightful girl, Miss Libby Hodges, of the Gardens staff.

27

Terrariums are within the reach of everyone and are fun to make. They are inexpensive and long lasting. Our son Tom made one in Cub Scouts that lasted several years.

A terrarium is a tiny garden in a clear glass or plastic container with a cover so that the moisture condenses and is re-used. Sometimes people make these little gardens in brandy snifters or other such containers and call them terrariums, but Miss Hodges, our expert, said that unless the container has a cover it is not a true terrarium, but a planter.

The first thing to do is to get your container, because obviously the size of container will influence the choice of plants. You may use almost anything and get it almost anywhere—your kitchen shelf, antique shops, the roadside. Miss Hodges' display included such varied containers as an old-fashioned cracker jar, a gallon vinegar jug, decorative whiskey bottles, fishbowls, commercially made terrarium containers, and many others. If the container you like doesn't have a cover, make one.

Miss Hodges preferred glass to plastic because it doesn't scratch and the collecting moisture stays in droplets rather than in a fog which might interfere with seeing the plants clearly. The container should be washed spotlessly clean and allowed to dry thoroughly so soil won't cling to the sides while you work.

Next, assemble your contents.

The first thing is small gravel the size of a pea which should be washed.

Second, get some activated charcoal, the kind you get from pet-fish shops, not the charcoal briquettes you use for outdoor cooking.

The third thing is the soil mixture made of 3 parts leaf mold, and 1 part perlite or vermiculite. You can substitute sand for the vermiculite.

Into the container put about an inch of the pea-sized gravel topped with ½ inch of charcoal, then add 1 inch or so of soil.

As you add the plants you will add more soil so that the soil-gravel-charcoal layers will take about one-third the container space. If you use small plants, this will give them growing room.

Now comes the fun part—selecting and placing the plants.

In a small container you may want to use only one plant, but in a larger one you will use two, three, or several, and they should be contrasting in texture and color. Include mosses and variegated plants, but unless your terrarium is very large, use only one variegated plant or you'll give your little garden a spotty look. Our lecturer suggested using native plants that you find on "plant hunts." These "plant hunts" should respect the plants on the endangered-species list. Never take a whole colony of plants even if they are not endangered. To be more protective of our native plants and shrubs confine the "hunts" to your own property. Some garden stores cater to terrarium owners by providing a supply of small plants that will more than meet your needs.

In addition to the two or three plants in your container, you can make a miniature landscape with rocks, singly or glued together to form hills and cliffs, pieces of wood, an empty snail shell, and other natural materials. She discouraged the use of live animals or china figurines.

Vary the soil level with slopes and valleys to make the surface look more natural. You can use ground covers such as moss, baby's tears, or lichens under the taller plants.

After you have everything arranged, clean the glass inside with a sponge and water the whole thing very, very lightly with a window-cleaner bottle or purchased sprayer using rain water or distilled water. If you use tap water, let it set for a day so the chemicals will settle. I doubt if you will see a pile of chemicals on the bottom of the jar but the surface will be free of them.

After you have planted and watered your terrarium, resist the urge to fertilize it. The organic matter in your planting medium will provide the necessary nutrients. You want to keep the growth slow so you won't have to be reworking the thing every few weeks. Don't hesitate to prune a plant if it becomes too large. Like outdoor shrubbery, the plant will soon recover and be the better for the pruning.

Put on the top.

Don't place your terrarium in direct sun or you'll make an oven from your airtight container and roast all the plants. It needs indirect light in a location that doesn't go much over 70°.

Sometimes you may find your container has too much moisture. Should this happen, remove the lid and with a sponge wipe off the collected droplets around the opening. You may also leave the opening uncovered for a bit to allow some evaporation.

If you want flowering plants, try African violets or one of the miniature orchids such as *Anoectochilus dowiananus*. Both do quite well in terrariums because of the controlled humidity.

Most folks, though, use only foliage plants of different textures, colors, and heights to create their little gardens.

Here are some plant combinations Miss Hodges used:

ebony spleenwort fern, *Dichondra*
wild violets, ebony spleenwort fern
walking fern, partridge berry, ebony spleenwort fern, British
    soldier lichen
baby's tears, miniature ivy
ruffly peperomia, asparagus fern, *Tradescantia*
dwarf *Euonymus*, rainbow moss
strawberry begonia
asparagus fern, rainbow moss, caladium
pine seedling, reindeer moss, British soldier lichen

As you can see, there are many combinations of plants to use depending on the size of the container.

I was at Peggy Pennell's house the other day for a Camp Fire Girls meeting and she had made the prettiest terrarium. It was quite large, 16 or 18 inches in diameter and beautifully planted, mostly with local flora. She used two purchased houseplants, one upright one and the other of a bush growth. The other plants included wild ginger, several small ferns, a little red-stemmed plant she couldn't identify, and moss, all from her nearby wood. She had also added a piece of aged wood and several small rocks to make a lovely little garden.

Your terrarium will last many months with almost no care. If a leaf does become yellow, prune it. If a plant gets too large, replace it.

Terrariums are fun. Make one.

Fourth Week
HOUSEPLANTS

Almost every house has what is supposed to be a green plant around somewhere. Sometimes the survival of such flora is doubtful and the descriptions of these indoor gardening attempts run all the way from luxuriant flowering specimens to poor, sick, yellowed, drooping things that look as if their next breath of carbon dioxide would be their last.

During my visit to the Indoor Gardening Seminar at Callaway Gardens one of our speakers talked about the general culture of houseplants.

He didn't come right out and say that the people who claim their plants grow well because they talk to them are not telling the truth. Instead he suggested that people who care enough for their plants to engage them in conversation were the same ones who accompanied the talking with watering, spraying, fertilizing, pruning, and other good garden practices.

This particular speaker emphasized what every gardener knows—the secret of growing houseplants or any other kind of plants successfully is to give them care. I suppose the same philosophy could apply to husbands, children, and guinea pigs.

In addition to this general admonition he had several more specific suggestions.

The first was to select plants that can live in the climate of your home. Not many families accustomed to central heating want to live in a house of 65°, the temperature preferred by most houseplants.

He suggested that many homes, because of the high temperature and low humidity, were better suited to the growing of cacti than foliage plants.

Fortunately many plants can adapt to the temperature of the average house. That they don't have ideal growing conditions is a blessing; otherwise, they would be putting out optimum growth and your living room would soon look like Tarzan's lair.

In a similar lecture at another time and place the speaker suggested that because the indoors is such an unnatural environment for plants most of them die sooner or later and that our goal should be to select plants that die slowly!

After selecting plants which more or less suit your house's temperature and humidity, he next offered water as the most important factor. He contended that as many plants are killed from over-watering as under-watering.

It is important to know the kind of water treatment plants need. Some such as dish gardens, should be thoroughly soaked each week, then left alone until the following week.

Others, such as the philodendrons, perhaps the most commonly grown foliage plant, and begonias should get barely dry between waterings, and still others should get throughly dry to the touch before more water is added.

Many plants like a soil that is consistently moist and humusy, which may mean a daily watering. Into this group fall the palms, caladiums, coleuses, ferns, and crotons.

Our speaker also suggested regular spraying with a fine mist, which serves both as a watering and cleaning method.

Soil is important in houseplant culture, and there are two schools of thought about this. According to one authority, research is being made into using a mixture of equal parts of peat moss and perlite or vermiculite. Because neither of these has nutrients you have to add fertilizer regularly.

Another, and the most often used mixture, is the one recommended for terrariums—2 parts good humus soil, 2 parts peat- ,and 1 part perlite. As far as possible you want to have the soil free of weeds, but if some do slip in you can snatch out the sprouts while you are having your daily conversations.

Your plants also have certain light requirements. In general plants do better growing in windows facing south or west. Many don't have to have direct sunlight; indirect will do fine. Too much light could result in too rapid growth. None will grow in dark places.

There are two solutions to the problem of having plants in a dark room. The first is to grow your plants in a sunny location, then bring them into the living room or wherever for a short time, then exchange for another one. The second is to use an artificial light. The best such light is a combination of one-watt incandescent light to three watts of florescent light. There are also specially designed florescent lights for growing plants.

Plants do best if they receive 16 hours of light each day, but they will do well with 12 to 14 hours. There are helpful little timers for turning the lights on and off.

Use fertilizer with a light hand. Our speaker recommended a slow-release kind so you don't have to keep all those little charts to remind yourself to feed plant A every second week and plant B every third week, etc.

The culture aim for houseplants is to keep them healthy but growing slowly.

Fourth Week
SPRING VEGETABLES

"Ed," I said to my husband as he left for the seed store, "One plants soybeans by the acre. One plants vegetables by the row."

When it's harvest time I lean toward the latter. My Ed's vegetable-planting practice leans toward the former. My profound announcement fell on deaf ears. The problem is that my Ed is a good gardener and likes to grow things. He goes into a seed store a perfectly sane man and leaves with enough seeds and plants to cover half the county.

Whatever size vegetable garden your interest, needs, and space dictate the first thing to do in planning each year's garden is to go to the Extension Office in your county. Each state's Extension Service annually publishes a manual listing the planting dates and recommended varieties of vegetable, fruits, etc., for your section of the state.

If rain, cold or other activities prevent your getting the seed sowing and plant setting done at the recommended time a delay of a week or so will be all right. Don't plant earlier than recommended.

Vegetables can be divided into groups depending on their cold tolerance and this determines their planting time.

The hardy vegetables which include cabbages, broccoli, beets, cauliflowers, onions, lettuce and carrots can be planted during the first two weeks in March or even earlier if you are sure and certain the late winter is going to stay mild.

Tender vegetables normally go into the ground the last two weeks of April. These include green bush beans, pole beans, sweet corn, and cantaloupes.

Tender vegetables that shouldn't be planted until the first or second week in May include lima beans, pole limas, eggplants, cucumbers, okra, peanuts, southern field peas, peppers, summer and winter squash, watermelons and tomatoes.

34

Be wise in the amount of these you choose to plant. You may need several rows of beans but only a few pepper plants will suffice. Son Bart thinks one eggplant plant is adequate for the entire Western Hemisphere.

You can wait as late as mid-June to plant sweet-potato slips and southern field peas and they will still do well. Always plant as early as the temperature will allow to get ahead of the insects.

Some vegetables should be planted at intervals. The threat of divorce hung heavily over our household one year when my Ed planted eight long rows of sweet corn at one time. These would have best been planted two rows at a time at two-week intervals to make the fresh corn season longer. The repeated plantings also mean that all the corn destined for the freezer doesn't demand attention at the same time.

Bush green beans do well with an early and a late planting.

The care and tending of a vegetable garden is not something you do in the spring and forget. A proper garden should have producing crops growing in it almost all year. This is achieved by paying attention to successive cropping, that is, immediately plant a second crop as soon as the first one is harvested.

Vegetable plots should get full sun. They also need water to produce fruit whether this "fruit" is a pod of okra, a seed inside a bean shell, or a cantaloupe. Make early preparations for ways to water your garden if the rains don't come. A delay in watering may mean a decided decrease in production. Watering methods are a matter of choice but many gardeners use the trickle irrigation system which uses minimum water with maximum effect.

You should consider mulching your vegetables if your plot is of a manageable size. Hoe the weeds a few times to destroy as many weed seeds as possible though of course you won't get them all. When the vegetables are about 6 to 10 inches high give them a heavy mulch with straw, leaves, well-decayed sawdust, wood chips, or whatever you have. You can use newspapers and magazines but be sure they are anchored so that they won't blow all over the neighborhood. This mulch helps eliminate weeds and to retain the moisture. If you follow this mulching practice every year in only a few years your soil will be loose and friable from the decay of the mulching material.

This mulch also keeps the vegetables cleaner for harvest. Anyone who has picked green bush beans after a rain has spattered soil all over them will instantly recognize this as a bonus.

Some home gardeners use the porous materials such as Spun Bond as a mulch. They last almost forever. They allow water to enter but weeds can't come through. The disadvantage is that they do not contribute to the organic improvement of the soil as the decomposing mulches do.

Don't plant too large a garden. If you don't plan to freeze and can, don't waste your seeds and labor by overplanting.

Notes for February

March

First Week
FERNS

Every farmhouse with a porch and a resident Farmer's Wife worth her salt should have at least two lush, green, healthy, gracefully flowing ferns by the door.

I recall a visit several years ago with my late aunt by marriage, Mrs. Auree McPhail, who was a pleasant part of the wedding package. Every year her porch held several of the most beautiful ferns. Delightful and energetic, she had grown ferns for 50 years and knew a lot about them. She loved the fishtails the most.

Ferns have many uses. They can be used out of doors in shady areas in the yard, under trees, beside buildings, along shaded walks. If you prefer growing them in pots you can sink the whole pot in the ground then lift it in the fall.

They can be used as full-time indoor plants if you have an apartment without access to porch or patio, and they make useful greenhouse plants both in pots and in hanging baskets.

Most people in the Piedmont follow the practice of my Aunt Auree using them as pot plants in the outdoors during summer then bringing them inside during the winter months.

She began her annual fern adventures in the early spring by separating and repotting those that had spent the winter inside. She always used fresh soil when repotting. A fern does best in a pot that is not too large, but it shouldn't be allowed to become potbound either.

Her potting medium was a mixture of leaf mold or woods' earth, good garden soil, well-rotted manure, and a little sand. The mixture makes a humusy, loose soil that stays moist and gives the tiny roots plenty of easy growing room.

Into her pot she first placed gravel or pebbles then added the soil mixture until it was the level at which the roots should start. She then added the plant and filled around it with the soil, adding a little sand in the immediate root area. The crown should be even with the top of the soil and leave about an inch of pot above to serve as a water catcher.

She also fertilized at potting time, using 3 or 4 tablespoons of complete fertilizer snitched from the barn supply. She put this around the extreme edge of the pot, watered the plant thoroughly, and it was on its way. In the absence of field fertilizer you can use any complete houseplant food or liquid manure to keep your fern lush.

Throughout the summer she fed the ferns, and when I asked her how often, she answered, ". . . whenever I look at them and they look as if they ought to be doing better." She never allowed the soil to dry. This meant that in the hottest part of summer she had to water about every other day in the late afternoon.

She placed hers so that they received morning sun, but if the day were extremely hot she moved them to the shaded part of the porch.

A fern should be given plenty of space. The fronds break easily if they are pushed against another plant or brushed by a passerby. Because the long, graceful, sweeping fronds are the real beauty of the plant, short, blunt, broken ends greatly detract from its appearance. Sometimes it is necessary to put the pot on a stand so the fronds will not touch the floor.

A hint for beautiful ferns is to keep them clean. If they are outside this is easily enough done with a water hose and a mist nozzle, but if they are inside in a huge pot that weighs a ton then other means must be devised.

Another favorite of fern growers is fluffy ruffles, *Nephrolepis exalatia bostoniensis*. This dwarf Boston is a bright-green plant with short fronds characterized by ruffles along the frond edges. Two other charming and often-grown plants are *Asparagus plumosa* and *Asparagus sprengeria*. These are sometimes called asparagus ferns but they aren't ferns at all; they are forms of ornamental asparagus grown from seeds, cuttings, or root divisions.

42

If you don't care for any of these there are more than 6,000 other members of the fern family from which you can choose.

If you have a spot in your yard that gets only speckled sun, try planting it with ferns then add a few white blooming plants such as white impatiens, and you'll discover that in mid-summer it is the coolest looking spot in your yard.

Second Week
ROSES

The opportunity a mother has to influence and mold the little lives in her keeping is overwhelming. The following conversations have recently occurred in our house:

"Mother, which shoes shall I wear with this dress?"

"I think the blue ones will look best."

"I'm going to wear my sneakers." And then there was this:

"Mother, should I take horticulture or woodworking for a 4-H project?"

"I think horticulture would be useful."

"I've decided to take farm mechanics."

And finally:

"Mother, should I have Laura or Pam to spend the night?"

"I think Pam. You owe her an overnight."

"I believe I'll ask Ann."

So I went out and viewed my roses, which looked as if cremation would solve all their problems. The little yellowed, spindly things stared pitifully at me, silently begging for mercy killing.

I telephoned W. C. Ripley, superintendent of parks for our city, which has two magnificent rose beds in one of its parks. One bed of 150 plants of the Doctor's Wife variety was given the city by the Medical Auxiliary. In the other bed, the 300 plants include more than 20 mixed varieties, all hybrid tea roses.

Mr. Ripley offered some suggestions for rose culture not always in agreement with rose growers, but a look at the beautiful display his beds make will prove his methods work.

In planting new beds he said his crew adds about a 1-pound-sized coffee can of basic slag mixed into the soil at the bottom of the hole and a cup or two of bone meal mixed with the other soil. This basic slag is a waste product created in the separation of iron from its ore. It is usually packaged in 40-pound bags and available at most garden stores. It is rich in trace elements especially iron and is an excellent soil additive. No other fertilizer, humus, or anything else is added. Roses require a sweet soil, Mr. Ripley contends, and this will keep them going the first year.

Each year thereafter he feeds them once or twice using a commercial rose fertilizer. He urges growers to follow the directions on the bag for the feeding schedule. He also gives each plant its canful of basic slag, but because this is not a fertilizer it can be done most anytime.

And right now in March you should get your roses pruned if you haven't done so, but Mr. Ripley is way ahead of you.

In the autumn after the first frost, they cut the plants back to about knee high so that wind whipping the tall growth won't heave the plants from the ground. Then in late February or early March before new growth starts, they will begin selective pruning, removing deadwood and undesirable canes, leaving three to five strong canes about a foot high.

Then, when the new growth begins and the leaves are about half an inch long, he begins the spraying which continues throughout the summer until November.

The two major enemies of roses are tiny aphids and fungi in the form of black spot and mildew. Both of these are prevented by weekly spraying, soaking the plant, and leaving it so wet that some spray drips onto the ground. Mr. Ripley emphasized the importance of spraying under the leaves. If you have only a few plants, he says dust can work as well, but spray is easier and better for a large garden. The aphids and fungi must never be allowed to start. And for that reason he opposes mulch on roses, although many folks swear by it. He says the fungi breed in the soil and he likes to keep the ground exposed so the sunshine can fight the fungus growth.

"We keep our roses clean," he said, adding that all prunings, leaves, and blooms are picked up. At the weekly spraying blooms are cut right above a branch that has five leaves, and the blooms are carried to local nursing homes. Mr. Ripley and his crew allow no one else to cut the roses and cautions against leaving blooms on the bushes because if they are allowed to form "apples" or hips, the plants will go dormant.

Did you know that during World War II many Britons ate cooked rose hips because of the high vitamin C content? This knowledge is from my store of unimportant facts.

Anyway, the weekly spraying keeps the plants healthy to insure well-developed, healthy blossoms.

If the sun comes down too long without rain, he sets about watering using a slow stream to thoroughly soak the ground around each bush. He warns against letting the water hit the leaves. Remove your hose nozzle and let the water flow directly onto the ground.

So I thanked Mr. Ripley, returned to my weedy little rose bushes, and uttered sweet reassurances. With some better care along the lines of Mr. Ripley's suggestions maybe I can mold and influence them.

Although the planting Mr. Ripley supervised didn't have any, there has been in the last few years a surge of interest in old roses. Five years ago it was difficult to find a source for "old roses," but now many catalogs are offering plants described as "old English roses," "species roses," "old fashioned roses," "old shrub roses," etc. These shrub roses are the results of crossing and usually are not the very same plant that great-great-grandmother grew in her yard.

There are several advantages to growing these roses. They are very fragrant and are long lived. They, of course, require care, but they are more disease resistant and generally more tolerant of soil and climate than their more temperamental relatives the hybrid teas. Most varieties bloom only once instead of twice or intermittently as do the teas, and they don't have that beautiful pointed bud form the hybrid teas have. They are useful plants, however, and if you love roses you'll want some of the "new" old roses in your garden.

Third Week
GOURDS

Frankly, I've always found it a little difficult to be serious about gourds. Perhaps it's a result of my South Georgia upbringing when we referred to a simple or inexperienced fellow as being "as green as a gourd."

Actually, gourds are the victim of a bad press. They are much more useful than, say, Swiss chard, which can only be eaten and that's the end of it. Gourds, on the other hand, can be used as residences for birds, water dippers, hanging flower containers, baby rattles, and purely for decoration when arranged in a large basket or bowl.

My expert on gourd culture, although he denies such a title, is Harry Gillespie, who has been growing gourds for years. I first knew Harry when I lived in his town several years ago. He is a thoroughly pleasant person and he cheerfully shared his gourd knowledge.

Because of the long growing season in most of the Piedmont, gourds can be planted directly in the garden a couple of weeks after frost or about the time you would plant their cousins, cucumbers and watermelons. If you want to be an early bird you can start the seed inside but that seems like a lot of bother when they grow so well by waiting and planting them outdoors.

Although they can be planted as late as June and still mature, Harry suggests early planting because insects become a problem with the late-planted ones.

The seeds should be planted in full sun about 1 inch deep and 2 or 3 feet apart to give them plenty of growing room. They'll cover half the country, so give them space. They don't require extremely rich soil; average garden soil is fine. You may want to enrich it some with compost, well-rotted manure, or a complete fertilizer if you think the soil needs such.

You can plant gourds to climb fences or trellises and their tiny tendrils will quickly catch onto the support. There are advantages to having them on the fence. They stay cleaner and won't decay from being on the ground during heavy rain, not that we have much of that in the summer.

Gourds require very little care. If you let them sprawl over the ground, you should keep out the weeds, but after awhile the leaves will shade out any weeds. Harry likes to quote one gourd grower who said if he worked gourds they would die! That ought to tell you something about their easy culture.

To preserve them, gourds should be harvested in the late summer or fall on a very dry day when they are thoroughly mature. Knowledge of when this is comes with experience, but generally the gourd will feel dry and the stem will be shriveled. Cut, leaving about an inch of stem on the gourd.

If you pick them too early, they'll decay; if you wait until they are too dry, they will lose their bright green, yellow, and white colors. Harry cautions to handle them gently like eggs. Don't go tossing them about.

Next he washes them in warm, soapy water, rinses them well, then lays them in the shade to dry. Other gourd growers prefer a solution of 1 part clorine bleach and 9 parts water. After a few days or "whenever I get around to it," he covers them with a coat of clear shellac. You can also use plain liquid self-polishing floor wax. Both enhance the gourds' bright colors and provide a protective coating. He has also used the paint youngsters use for plastic models to paint designs on faded gourds or to highlight their colors. Because some gourds grow in rather peculiar shapes you can use this method to develop whimsical animals or decorations.

There are many kinds of gourds. Harry suggests the beginner buy a package of mixed ornamentals. You can also save seed from other years.

If you want to be more selective in your gourd enterprises, they are generally grouped into (1) small ornamental or *Ovifera* gourds and (2) the large ones, *Lagenaria*. They include such names as white pear, nest egg, ringed pear, turban, spoon, and powder horn and range in size from a few inches to the snake gourd that grows to 10 feet, although what you would do with that one after you grew it I'm sure I don't know.

The three most commonly grown ones are probably the small ornamentals, usually polished and used for winter decorations; the bottle gourds, commonly used for martin houses; and the siphon or dipper gourds that our great-grandpappies kept hanging beside the water bucket. Some folks say you can alter the shape of the dipper gourd by wrapping a tape around its neck when it is small.

Harry has won ribbons and prize money at the fair for his gourds, in addition to enjoying them all winter for their bright, shiny colors.

Even if you don't have a green thumb, try gourds. They'll grow for anybody. And should you get serious about them, there is an enthusiastic gourd group you can join. They'll tell you how to grow bigger and better gourds. Please see listing at end of book.

Fourth Week
PREPARING SOIL

I would like to take issue officially with the fellow who said, "If it's worth doing at all it's worth doing right," or something like that. Now that just isn't true.

Take, for instance, making beds. Although getting them made every day is an accepted household practice, it isn't really necessary to have the corners mitered and the sides tucked in. To my knowledge, unless it was one especially nosey cousin, no one has ever checked my bed to make sure I had mitered my corners.

But there are times when doing something right is very important, and the preparation of garden soil is one of them.

Sunday, some of the children and I went for a bike ride. It was a ride for them. For me it was a ride, a walk, a push—depending on the terrain. Our dog went along gathering his dog friends at every house so that we made a rather interesting parade near the end of our route with the riding and the pushing, plus the barking of several dogs of assorted sizes, colors, and genders.

The flowering wild plum, the red-winged blackbird, and the yards full of daffodils said again what I had suspected for a week, it was time to get busy in the yard. This doesn't mean you should rush out and plant everything this afternoon. In fact, my late gardening buddy and neighbor Pete Cooper, remembering late snows and frosts, always cautioned that anything planted too early, even in our wonderful Southland, risked a good chance of getting killed.

The first day you can pick up a handful of soil, squeeze it, and have it collapse when released instead of staying in a damp ball, you will know you are on your way.

The most important part of any gardening program, and this could be said a million times, is the preparation of the soil. You can get by without mitering your bed corners and no one will even know or care, but a shrub, plant, or seed put into improperly prepared soil will shout to all the world during its brief, weak life that you are a careless, ignorant, or lazy gardener, either of which is enough to condemn you.

This is worth doing right. Do it correctly now, and as you add things here and there throughout the spring, the chores will go much easier for you.

First you must determine if your soil texture is clay, sandy, or loam, and you can pretty well tell by looking at it. It can change from one section of the yard to another. One side of my yard has good soil; the other side looks like the raw material for a pottery factory.

If you visit your neighbors when they are sick and tithe regularly, then you may be rewarded with loam, that ideal mixture of sand, clay, and humus reserved for the pure in heart, and you should be eternally grateful. The rest of us will have to strive and struggle.

Both sandy and clay soils can be improved by the addition of humus. Remember, I told you to make a compost heap. Humus does all kinds of marvelous things to the soil, and according to one writer is "one of the most important factors in a program of good soil management." It increases the water-holding capacity by several hundred percent, it means greater aeration, decreases baking and crusting of the soil surface, allows more water storage for dry times, prevents leaching of soluble fertilizers, absorbs the sun's rays, which stimulate root growth in early spring, promotes bacterial action, and all kinds of other good things. I just don't see how you can get along without it.

Having established its virtues, we must next determine where to get this good stuff. The compost pile you should have going is the answer, but if you don't have one, there are other sources.

The quickest way is to buy peat from your garden store and

thoroughly dig it into the soil. Another source, requiring more work but less expense, is leaf mold from a wooded area. Although there will be a lot of fussing and quarreling about it, the collecting of this is a good job for children.

In addition to the humusy material, mix in any animal manure, preferably well rotted. It takes about a year for it to properly decompose, so start now for next year if you have to. Cottonseed meal, superphosphate, basic slag, wood ashes, and other materials that provide necessary nutrients can go in now.

Dig up the whole thing. If you are in a vegetable garden you can use a tiller easily, but if you are working beds and borders of small irregular shapes, the only way to do it is with a small spade and a large muscle.

The lightweight mini-tillers are excellent for this but they have their limitations. You cannot wade into hard, untilled ground with a mini-tiller. If the area has been dug previously the minis are great, leaving the soil marvelously pulverized and soft. Their small size allows them to get in areas and around plants where the large tillers are unmanageable.

An efficient way to dig and thoroughly mix soil is the process sometimes called "double digging." First dig a trench about a foot or so wide and a foot deep across one end of the border, and save the soil in a wheelbarrow for later use. Into the hole put the manure, humus, and other stuff. Dig the section next to it, putting the turned over soil on top of the humus, etc., in the hole. Fill the second trench, and so on, until the end of the bed is reached. The last hole is filled with the soil saved from the first. Go back over it a second time and spade it up good again and rake it smooth.

Assuming you are still alive after all this work, you are now ready to put out any perennial, annual, or seed. When the buying fever hits and you arrive home with a dozen flats of plants, you will be glad the soil is ready. All you have to do is dig a hole with your trowel and pop them in.

Try to do all this digging two or three weeks before planting time so the soil can settle. It will also give you time to settle. You're not a machine you know. You can't do it all in one day.

Fourth Week
LEGUMES

As soon as late cold snaps are over, threats of frost are gone and the ground warms, the home vegetable gardeners each year turn out in droves to plant their rows.

One group of vegetables that almost every gardener will plant is the legumes. We commonly call them beans and peas and they include dozens of varieties.

This group is a good choice for the home gardener. If space is limited use it to the maximum by planting crops that produce large amounts of real food. Don't tie up a small vegetable plot all summer to grow one pumpkin for Halloween unless that one pumpkin is your goal in life.

The word legume means that the fruit has a single-cavity ovary which splits along two seams when dry. The most remarkable thing about legumes, though, is their ability to take nitrogen from the air and adapt it to plant use. For this reason they are great soil builders.

Nutritionally they supply protein, calcium, and vitamins A and D and as foodstuffs for both man and farm animals they represent the cheapest form of digestible proteins and other nutrients. A half cup of cooked dried navy beans, for instance, provides seven grams of protein and we need only 45 to 65 grams a day.

Beans and peas are, without question, the most useful plants in your garden. Most of them can be eaten in the pod, as with green beans, or as a mixture of green "snaps" and shelled peas as with the southern field peas, as mature green beans such as the varieties of limas, or as fully mature dried beans. Most of the varieties can be canned, frozen, or dried.

Almost all the beans and peas have certain culture requirements in common. They all need sun, adequate but not excessive moisture, and neutral soil. If your soil is acid, add lime to get it as near to a neutral pH 7 as possible.

Most legumes require a soil temperature of 50° to 60° to germinate and will produce better yields if the temperature does not go over 85°. This is why the vines start looking droopy and stop producing when the July temperatures hit 90° or 95° even if there is adequate rain.

The soil into which you plant the seeds should be prepared to a depth of 10 to 12 inches. Work into it well-rotted manure or 0–10–0 superphosphate fertilizer.

Green beans, sometimes called snap beans, string beans or French beans are a garden favorite. They are tender annuals and should be planted when the soil warms usually during the first two weeks of April. Plant the seeds 3 to 6 inches apart, cover them with about 1½ inches of fine soil in rows 24 to 36 inches apart depending on whether you will cultivate with a hoe or tiller. If you are using a mini-tiller you may be able to plant them even closer. If you make the right choice to mulch heavily you can plant the rows so close that the mature bean plants almost touch. This close planting can add several rows to a small garden plot, but do leave enough space to move about for harvesting.

When several inches high, give the bean plants a side dressing of a complete fertilizer. Green beans usually produce in 50 to 60 days and the season can be easily extended by making successive plantings. There are several varieties of the half-runner beans. The culture is the same but you should allow more space between plants.

If you have a large vegetable garden and want to plant pole green beans I recommend the good advice of our friend Dave "Doc" Chastain. He plants the last week of April and uses the

Kentucky Wonder variety but agrees that many of the other newer varieties are as good or better. He begins with a 3-inch deep furrow which he sprinkles rather heavily with a commercial fertilizer such as 5–10–5, 4–12–12 or any of a similar analysis. He covers this with loose soil back to ground level. Next on top of this furrow he makes a V-shaped 1-inch-deep furrow. He plants his seeds rather thickly because he says he had rather thin the emerging seedlings than to replant. He covers the seeds with about ¾ inches of soil and waits for a good rain.

When the bean plants are a few inches high, Doc puts up the supports. In theory, he says laughing at himself; in practice the supports are usually left in the garden year round. These supports are 6-foot metal posts driven into the ground about 8 feet apart. Between the posts he stretches two horizontal lines of nylon cord, one at the top and the other at the bottom. At each bean plant he puts a vertical string connecting the upper and lower cords to provide the twining support.

He makes a dual attack against heat and drought. First, he uses well-rotted sawdust as a mulch. Second, he makes a little trench along the bean row and when the weather is driest he uses the hose to fill the trench with water. This constant supply of water is needed to keep the vines healthy and in production.

About mid-summer he gives the vines a top dressing with the same fertilizer used in the planting furrow.

Doc's pole beans usually produce for about three months dying in September.

Lima beans take longer to harvest time, usually 60 to 90 days after planting. The pole limas, like the pole green beans, produce more beans and for a longer period than do the bush varieties. Some growers say that when planting limas the "eye" should always be placed downward. We very laboriously planted a row like that one year and could see no difference in the harvest.

The butter pea is another favorite legume. This is a type of lima but cream colored, rounded and with a sweeter flavor.

The southern field peas including varieties of the cream and crowder peas are excellent garden vegetables. They require more space than green beans or limas but produce prolifically. We prefer them cooked with equal parts of shelled and snapped peas.

The home gardener can also grow kidney beans, pinto beans, black-eyed peas and many other varieties for drying but unless he has a really large garden area it is probably just as well to buy these.

Notes for March

April

First Week
SHADY GARDENS

About this time of year the gardener is bitten by the same bug at garden shops that infects the auction visitor—she buys everything in the store when she came only to look.

The flats of bedding plants now decorating store fronts are about as irresistible to the gardener as lemonade would be to a fellow lost in the Sahara. But the gardener with a shady yard quickly finds she has two problems. The first is trying to maintain some dignity while bending over reading labels of plants set flat on the sidewalk, and the second is discovering that most annuals in these flats require full sun.

We agree that if one had to choose between shade and flowers we would take the shade, but no such choice is necessary, because with some thought and planning the shady garden can be just as attractive and much cooler than the one in the sun.

Although there are annuals that will grow in partial shade, don't depend on them for your whole garden. Use perennials, biennials, and both spring and summer bulbs for the backbone of your shady spot and use the bright annuals for accents.

We have shade here at our house in the country, and my favorite plant for it is the impatiens, an improved strain of the old sultana that graced many a front porch as a pot plant. These are offered as seeds by most every seed house, but you get blooms much earlier if you buy the plants.

Impatiens have tender stems and demand lots of water. Each plant grows to a 2-foot size both in width and height and is sprinkled generously with flowers in shades of pink, red, orange, lavender, or white all summer. Because of their size, a few plants go a long way. There are also dwarf varieties for edging or for entire beds, and although they are useful, I prefer the big lush plant of the standard impatiens.

59

Another plant often used only as a pot plant but that is good as a shady garden resident is the fibrous begonia. I have used begonias with impatiens for a pretty bed. The only problem is that you have to spend the summer with water hose in hand.

Tuberous begonias not only live in partial shade but require it. To become really spectacular plants the tuberous begonia must have a good soil high in organic material. Use both well-rotted manure and material from the compost pile in your planting site. The tuber looks somewhat like a gladiolus corm and is planted with the scooped-out side up and barely covered. Don't put them out too early because they won't do anything until the soil warms. To get early blooms start the tubers indoors.

Another bulb that can be started now and moved outdoors is the caladium. You can put it directly into the ground, but it is likely to sit there for several weeks. The caladium will do well in a semi-shaded location, but some sun makes the leaves more colorful. This is also true of the coleus, another favorite, which will grow in both sun and shade.

Shady spots almost cry for ferns, and these too need much organic matter in the soil. They will need water but will reward you with a tropical atmosphere in your special shady garden.

Don't forget the hosta, sometimes called plantain lily or funkia. Although they do have a spiky blossom, their real glory is their large, shiny leaves. Give them plenty of room, for they will make a large mound. Plant them about 2 feet apart. There has been an explosion of interest in hostas in the last few years resulting in a large number of varieties of small, medium, and large plants to fit almost any shady garden need.

What would a garden in the shade be without day lilies? True, they produce their best blooms in sun, but they do well enough in partial shade for you to include them. They can be transplanted most anytime, require little care, bloom for a long period, and in general are adaptable plants. Neighbors will probably give you dozens if you happen to casually state you could use some day lilies.

There are several annuals that bloom fairly well in light shade. This means high tree branches with good air circulation. Hardly any annual will bloom in dense shade.

A list of shady bloomers includes petunias, pansies, snap-dragons, Chinese forget-me-nots, Drummond's phlox, sweet alyssum, and some salvias. Others that will endure even more shade are cockscomb, *Nicotiana* (flowering tobacco), lobelia, calendula, and stock. Both stock and *Nicotiana* have the added attraction of a lovely fragrance. Rudbeckia, although a peren-nial, will bloom the first season from seed in partial shade, so we shall include it.

Many of these flowers may not be available in plants be-cause they are not familiar and there has been no demand for them. Seed are available from the store and catalogs, and as their designation implies, these "annuals" will bloom this sum-mer if you plant this spring.

Don't get carried away with buying seed. Seed buying is an even more serious infection than plant buying because they are cheaper, and you'll buy more than you need thinking how clever and economical you are.

Remember one hard and fast rule of gardening: a small plot carefully planned and tended is much more attractive than a long border that is weedy and scraggly. Before you dig up the whole yard and sow seed right and left, remember last July's temperatures and consider how much time you are going to give your garden when the insanity of early spring wears off and the days get long, hot, and dry.

One final point about shady gardens: incorporate as many white flowers as you can into the bed. They make the whole area seem lighter and cooler in their contrast with the greens.

Second Week
TUBEROUS BEGONIAS

I had been the victim of bad advice, I concluded as I read the folder that came with my purchase of three begonia tubers for my hanging basket.

Several years earlier I had tried growing tuberous begonias in a planter that was in full sun most of the day after some well-intentioned friend who didn't know what she was talking about suggested, "You should use tuberous begonias here."

Being young in years and a mere babe in the matters of plants and flowers, I took myself down to the garden store and bought a pile of tubers that promised me a rainbow of loveliness. I planted them. They came up. They grew some. Then they all died.

What my friend had neglected to tell me was that the tuberous begonia, that beautiful queen of the shady garden, is a poor, pitiful thing in a sunny one, if it survives at all. My planter received sun most of the day. After a couple of years of failure, I changed to growing geraniums and petunias in it, and they did quite well—when I could remember to water them.

The tuberous begonia is a member of the family Begoniaceae which also includes the fibrous rooted begonia that bears clusters of flowers in panicles and the *Begonia rex* which, although it has flowers, is grown primarily for its colorful leaves.

Tuberous begonias are rather expensive, but they should last several seasons if you are careful and save them over winter. You can use them as pot plants indoors and on the porch and patio. If used inside, they must have light; don't put them in a dark corner. They can be grown out of doors directly in soil in a shady location.

Three things begonias must have are humusy soil, adequate moisture, and either partial or full shade. If you put them in full sun, you're condemning the poor things. They make lovely pot plants for a tree-shaded patio and do as well in the open shade of a porch. The trailing kinds are especially good for hanging baskets, but you must remember that baskets need watering more frequently because they are exposed to drying air on all sides.

The directions say to start the plants in early spring by putting the saucer-shaped tubers, hollow side up, close together, in a shallow box of peat and sand. The sprout comes from the center of the hollow. After they start growing and get about 3 inches high, transplant to peat pots, then, when the weather is warm, put the peat pots in the ground outside. You can plant the tubers directly in the ground, but they require a temperature not lower than 60° to 65° to sprout, and if you wait until the nights are that warm your begonia blooms will be late coming.

If you are planning to use them in pots or hanging baskets, you can start them directly in these containers. Barely cover the tuber, keep it moist and out of direct sun. When it gets some growth, give it liquid fertilizer. This should be continued every couple of weeks all during the season for both the pot plants and those grown in the garden.

Don't crowd the plants. Usually one tuber to a medium-sized pot is enough. In a large hanging basket you can use two or three of the cascading ones to be sure of having a full, overflowing basket instead of a plant perched over on one side.

When the first buds appear, pick them off. Although you may not want to do so, this will make the plant stronger. After the plant gets large and sturdy, let the buds stay. They will bloom from May or June until frost. As the blooms fade and a leaf dies, pick them off to encourage more blooms.

The bloom of the tuberous begonia is like a flat camellia. The bloom may be single or double and some have fringe-edged petals. Each blossom is a lovely thing by itself, and expert begonia growers tell us that they should be grown where they can be seen up close so the real beauty of the flower can be appreciated. The bright, vivid colors of the blooms are the flower's biggest asset. These extremely brilliant colors include yellow, coral, pink, red, and almost all flower colors, except blue and lavender-blue.

If your begonias are outdoors, the first frost will get them. When this happens, remove the dead stalk, shake the soil from the tuber, and let the tuber dry in the sun a few days. Then store it someplace, preferably in dry sand or peat, until next February or March when you start all over again.

One thing you may have to do is to stake the plant. Each bloom lasts a long time and the heavy bloom plus the large stalk is sometimes too much for the shallow roots. At planting time put in a stake, pushing it all the way to the bottom of the pot, and as the plant grows tie it gently to the already provided stake, which will hardly show among the large leaves.

There are several problems that can beset begonias, but I'm not going to tell you about them. If you know about them, you might start having them, especially if you have any hypochondriac tendencies. In general, good, humusy soil, plenty of water, and shade will produce healthy plants. Some folks say tuberous begonias are hard to grow. My experience is that whether something is hard to grow depends on how much care you give it and the climatic conditions. A weed would be hard to grow if the seed were planted among rocks and never received any water or nourishment.

If you are determined to do so, you can increase your number of tuberous begonias by taking softwood cuttings. So far I have resisted this urge. Cut straight across the stem below a node and coat the newly cut end with a rooting compound. Put it in damp sand, keep it in the shade, and in a few weeks roots should develop. On the other hand, they may not. In that case you go buy another tuber, which would probably have been the simplest thing in the first place.

The brilliantly colored tuberous begonias are lovely for brief indoor visits. If they are in pots bring them inside for a party or special occasion then return them to the porch or patio.

There are few flowers that bloom over a longer period—six or seven months—than the tuberous begonia. If you've never grown tuberous begonias, buy at least one this year.

As the man says, "Try it. You'll like it."

Third Week
COLEUS

When the water got deeper outside my window last Saturday, as is the nature of April Saturdays, my face got longer and my disposition got grouchier when I thought of my poor lettuce plants languishing in their paper bag instead of being happily settled in a garden row. So, as a do-it-yourself booster-upper, I turned from thoughts of unplanted vegetable seed and lettuce plants to the mental image of my beautiful flower garden this summer.

Not heeding my own advice, I have purchased enough flower seed to plant an entire state rather than one yard. Something I want to try from seed for the first time this year is the coleus. My mother always grew coleuses as pot plants for the porch. I couldn't see much in them. Their dark, reddish-brown colors were really not very uplifting to the spirits.

But like virtue, sobriety, and thriftiness, the coleus is one of the old things whose value has remained constant, even improved. It is enjoying new popularity as a foliage plant, and well it should, because the dark, dull colors of other years have given way to brilliant, clear, light colors at the hands of the developers.

Most of our bush plants are descendents of *Coleus blumei,* a native of Java, and the trailing one is a "grandchild" many times removed from *Coleus rehneltianus* of Ceylon.

Once limited almost entirely to pot-plant culture, the coleus is finally coming into its own and is found in almost every part of the garden: borders, beds, edgings for drives, pot plants for porch and patio, window boxes, terrariums, as a filler among small, young shrubs, and even for water culture.

There is one variety, Trailing Queen, that does well in hanging baskets. Although I know about it, I don't know where to get it. I have checked several seed catalogs, but none offer it.

The coleus, because of its agreeable way of growing in the shade, has often been left there. Although it will grow there without complaining, to reach its full beauty and most brilliant color it should get some sun. If the temperature does not stay too high for too long and if the plants get adequate water, they can be planted in full sun.

And what colors there are! Several years ago the chartreuse was developed, and it makes a spectacular bed by itself. There are vivid shades of pink, salmon, red, white, green, and yellow. Try coleuses as a background for a lower plant that repeats some of its colors for a color feast.

The usual growth is about 20 inches, but there are dwarf varieties that reach only 8 to 10 inches. With this range you can find many places for it in the border.

It is better pinched back to maintain a bushy growth. You can do this by pinching the very tip or by allowing the branch to get longer and snipping off enough for a cutting. The coleus does have a bloom but it's nothing to write home about—a little blue spike of a thing that is better removed so that the plant will develop showy leaves.

The bright plants require warm weather, humusy soil, and plenty of water. It is one of the first victims of frost and the first plant to wilt from a shortage of moisture. It can serve as a signal flower that your whole bed needs watering.

Coleuses are available in spring either in flats or peat pots. If you decide to grow them from seed, start them indoors in March or April so they'll be large enough to put outside when the weather promises, on Scout's honor, to be finished with frost.

The usual way of propagating the coleus is to take cuttings. Cut the stem at the node (that's the fat place along the stem where the new leaves pop out) and plant it in damp sand. The sand should be kept damp, and in about three weeks the cutting will have a root system developed enough to go outside. You can root them in water, but the roots get all tangled and the sand method is better.

If your plant is in a pot, when frost threatens this fall you can bring it inside and enjoy it all winter. Next spring you can take cuttings for new plants and you're on your way again.

You can grow the plant entirely in water, but you should add a drop or two of liquid plant food occasionally so it won't starve.

Coleus plants' availability vary from those with 1- or 2-inch leaves to those with large 10-inch leaves. Some are slightly serrated and others are deeply fringed and notched, giving a lacy effect. These brightly colored leaves are useful in arrangements or in collections by themselves.

Take your coleus out of the shade and put it in your sunniest location for a summer-long display of spectacular color.

Fourth Week
EDGING PLANTS

The unequaled, magnificent Piedmont spring is here bringing with it the planning, planting, and burrowings of the eager gardener.

This planning should include some thought of edging plants. An edging plant is one that "edges," separating a walk, drive, or border from another part of the yard.

If your garden is in a natural setting it probably won't need an edging because the yard blends into the woodland area without too much obvious separation. However, if yours is a town lot or a farm home where you want to clearly mark property lines or areas, then you are probably using a fence, hedge, or border of some kind that will require an edging.

The low, compact edging plants are used in many places. They often front the foundation shrubs around the house, and can be used in front of a shrub border such as deciduous shrubs or azaleas. They serve to separate the lawn area from flower beds and borders. Sometimes the edging is the whole thing, such as a narrow row of low plants or flowers along a drive or walk.

Edgings can be other than flowers. You can lay brick in front of your shrubbery border, use a mulch of pebbles kept neatly in place, set landscape timbers or other lumber or rocks flush with the ground. All of these serve as a dividing line.

Edgings give a finished look to a yard. If the same edging material is used to front a long winding border, a large variety of flowers within the border can be united with harmony. This continuous row of plants of the same kind gives your garden order. It doesn't look as if you just went out and put all your plants in one place and left.

Edgings can be low shrubs, annuals, perennials, grasses, or even vines. An edging plant should first of all be quite low and compact in growth, not more than 6 or 8 inches tall. If it is in front of tall flowers or shrubs, of course, it can be taller, but generally a low 4- to 6-inch plant makes a better appearance. It should be compact in growth with flowers or foliage going from the ground to the top. Avoid plants with leggy stems even if they are short. Edging plants should be fairly hardy because you will use a large number of them, and you don't want something you have to pamper all the time.

If you select a blooming annual or perennial, choose one that has a long blooming season or plan to replace an early bloomer with a later blooming plant.

If you want to keep your foundation planting evergreen you might consider several varieties of *Juniperus horizontalis* including *Juniperus horizontalis douglaii* called Waukegan Juniper and a smaller form *Juniperus horizontalis procumbnes* and any of the other dwarf shrubs.

Ornamental grasses are often used, including the evergreen liriope, which ranges in color from dark green to green-and-white and green-and-yellow striped. The ivies make good evergreen edgings but have to be kept trimmed or they too will take over the bed. In fact, I hesitate to recommend them because as attractive as ivy is in a neat row it is a high-maintenance plant if it is kept trimmed. Any of the varieties of santolina make neat 12-to-18 inch mounds of green or gray-green foliage. Santolina does not require pruning.

Both ivy and the ornamental grasses make good edgings for walks and drives because they stay there and don't have to be reset each year. The leaves of the grass falling onto a neatly clipped lawn are rather pleasing to the eye.

If you prefer annuals, you can still have a foliage plant. Choose a coleus, but keep it pinched to make a low bushy plant. For blooming plants, you can choose among dwarf ageratum, sweet alyssum, dwarf snapdragons, dwarf calendula (sometimes called pot marigold), dwarf celosia, dianthus, candytuft, *Phlox drummondii,* nasturtiums, verbena, dwarf marigolds, lobelia, and dwarf zinnias.

Some perennials you might like are maiden pink dianthus, coral bells, evergreen candytuft, Iceland poppy, and cushion mums.

If you haven't been using an edging to unify your garden plan, do so this year. You'll like the ordered effect.

Notes for April

May

First Week
MARIGOLDS

During the 30 years my Ed served in our state legislature I constantly urged him to introduce legislation requiring every resident of our state with land the size of a pocket handkerchief to plant at least one packet of marigold seeds. Since my political influence with him ranged somewhere between none and not at all he never did so.

The fight for proper recognition of the marigold, sometimes called the "Friendship Flower," was led for many years by the late Senator Everett Dirksen who wanted to make it the national flower. I have never known why folks disagreed with him. It is true that the marigold is not native to the continental United States. Most of them come from Mexico or South America but that would be appropriate because except for the American Indian we all came from somewhere else also. The marigold possesses many of the virtues a good American should have: it is sturdy, healthy, and attractive; it can survive even in unpleasant surroundings; it is undemanding; it is independent, requiring only the basics of sun, water, and fair soil; and it is productive.

Although the catalogs list them as either African (*Tagetes erecta*) for the tall ones, or French (*Tagetes patula*) for the dwarf double ones, both kinds of marigolds originated in Mexico and are therefore native to our North American continent.

Because of its popularity and easy culture, the marigold has been a favorite subject for horticulturists to improve, and one seed dealer lists 61 kinds of marigold seed, varying from the 6-inch dwarf with 1-inch blossoms to a 4-footer boasting 5-inch blooms. Therefore, anyone who cannot find a marigold to suit him is just too hard to please and is probably also difficult to live with.

Although I have always rather liked the pungent scent of the marigolds, some people object to them and our horticulturist buddies have jumped in and produced many varieties that are odor free.

The colors of marigolds range from near white through bright, clear, lemon yellow to the oranges and almost true reds. It is almost slothful for anyone with a yellow or white color scheme in any room not to grow a big bed of marigolds to keep that room in flowers all summer.

The uses of marigolds are multiple. Unsurpassed as edging plants, low rows of the dwarf plants can tie an entire border together with beauty and neatness. Most French dwarfs are compact with blooms almost covering the plants from the time they start blooming in mid-June until frost. For several years I have used the petite lemon drop around our front with good effect.

The tall varieties make a bright background for other mid-sized annuals and perennials. Because of the weight of the flower heads they may need staking, but the results are worth the effort. Plant the large ones about 18 inches apart, and the small ones 8 to 9 inches apart. Although they don't require a rich soil, they will benefit from mulching, especially during long dry spells. Soil that is too rich especially in nitrogen can be bad because it will produce more foliage and less flowers.

If you have a sunny space, make a cutting garden with rows of different kinds of marigolds to give you armfuls of flowers all summer for your house, your neighbors, the church, and passing vacuum cleaner salesmen.

Marigolds can be massed in beds by themselves. Several years ago I was in a little community in a neighboring state, and the roadside held several large beds measuring 50 square feet or more filled with marigolds in full bloom. The effect was spectacular.

My good friends the marigolds can be used in window boxes, hanging baskets, planters, as narrow edgings for walks and drives, in pots and tubs for the porch or terrace, or just about any place else a gardener fancies. Because of its undemanding culture, it is the lazy gardener's plant. One would be hard put to find a more agreeable flower for size and color variations and easy growth.

You can buy flats of plants that will give you earlier blooms, but unless there is some special reason why you must have these early blooms, such as a visit from rich Uncle Henry, it seems sort of spendthrifty to buy marigold plants when they are so easy to grow from seeds.

Sow them in early May. If you plant them much earlier, they will probably rot in the cold, wet soil. If the weather is warm enough and the soil damp enough, they will germinate in about a week. With favorable conditions the dwarf ones will begin blooming in about six weeks.

You'll probably plant them too thickly, which is just as well, because they transplant quite easily when they are about 2 inches high. This way you can get them exactly where you want them, and pinching out the tip to make up for any lost roots will help prevent wilting at transplanting time.

Although they will struggle along in partial shade, they will do their top blooming if given full sun and adequate water. They will withstand drought better than most annuals, but they need water in the driest times.

To enjoy maximum blooming period, plant the seed this month, but they may be planted any time during the summer and will bloom prolifically until frost. Like many other annuals, they benefit from having their old blooms removed. This allows the plant to direct its energies toward making new blooms rather than producing seed in the wilted ones.

A healthy plant, the marigold's only real enemies are the red spider mite and the tarnished plant bug, an ugly little thing about ¼-inch long that can be controlled with Sevin spray. Usually even this is not necessary.

For a bright display and easy growth, no flower surpasses the marigold. Both Senator Dirksen and I said so.

Second Week
FRAGRANT FLOWERS

The reason most of us plant flowers and shrubs is because they're pretty. But if they smell good too, then that's a bonus.

There are many flowers that provide pleasant fragrance as well as lovely blooms, and to gain more pleasure from her garden the beginning gardener should include some of these in her garden planning.

There are many places where fragrant plants are useful. The first, perhaps, is at the entrance so that visitors get a favorable impression as they wait for you to answer the doorbell. These fragrances can be offered by shrubs, seasonal flowers, or even pot plants.

The second is in the area of outdoor living, whether outside a screened porch or around a terrace or patio. An informal sitting area, which is what most folks have, among the trees is much more inviting if there is a slight fragrance of flowers in the air.

Also desirable is having scented plants outside your eating or sleeping area so that the fragrance enters the windows. At another house we had a gardenia bush outside the bedroom window that provided pleasure all summer. Scented pot plants in sunny windows provide a freshness to the whole room.

One scented shrub I especially like is the sweet shrub. It is deciduous, so it doesn't look like much in fall and winter, but its spicy, brown blooms in spring and summer more than make up for its scraggly appearance in winter. Its real name is *Calycanthus floridus,* although it is more commonly called Carolina allspice, sweet shrub, or strawberry shrub. It looks like a bunch of sticks when the leaves drop, so don't use it as a foundation plant.

When I was a youngster, Betty Foster was a good friend of mine, and at the Foster house there was a tall shrub, porch-ceiling high, that they called banana shrub because of its inch-long, slender, pale-yellow buds that later opened into flat flowers. In the bud stage it had the most delicious banana smell, and ever since I have wanted a banana shrub.

The leader among fragrant shrubs is the lilac. There are several kinds of lilacs all producing fragrant clusters of blooms in white, blue, pink, or lavender. This is a case or do-as-I-say not do-as-I-do because I have not successfully grown the common lilac *Syringa vulgaris*. My neighbor almost in sight of my window grows beautiful fragrant ones. I have a Korean lilac Miss Kim which is lovely but it does not have the wonderful fragrance of the common lilac. Generally the common lilac prefers a temperate climate and does not do well in the areas of the Piedmont where the summers get really hot.

Still another king among the scented shrubs is the gardenia (*Gardenia jasminoides veitchi*) or Cape jasmine, as they are often called. Only two or three of the flat, white, waxy blooms can perfume a whole room. They are easily bruised, so don't touch the petals when you're collecting them.

Mock orange (*Philadelphus coronarius* and *Philadelphus virginallis*) is another fragrant plant with its little yellow-centered white flowers, but it doesn't compare with the gardenia. If you take off most of the leaves when you bring it inside, it will last longer.

Daphne, with its rose-colored blooms in spring and fall, provides fragrance. The old-fashioned abelia, which is covered in summer with small white or pink trumpet-shaped flowers, provides a pleasant aroma throughout the season. Some of the azaleas are scented.

Two vines that provide fragrance are wisteria and honeysuckle, the latter being among the most fragrant of all plants. Its sweet, distinctive scent can be detected some distance away, and one of the pleasures of summer is to ride by a fence row covered with honeysuckle and have its fragrance meet you through the open car window. Both of these shrubs should be planted with discretion, however, because they can get out of bounds quickly.

Flowering almond is another fragrant plant whose only recommendation is its tiny, tight, pink, double blossoms exploding for a short time in the spring. During the rest of the year there's not much that can be said for it.

Other fragrant plants include the herbs such as rosemary and lemon verbena, and that giant of the home grounds, the southern magnolia.

What list of fragrant shrubs would be complete without roses? As a rule, the old-fashioned roses are more fragrant than the hybrid teas, which often don't have any fragrance at all.

When you plan your garden, plant a few fragrant shrubs. You'll be glad you did.

Third Week
DAISIES

Saturday afternoon I went over to Susie's house to get the daisies she had offered me. She gave me some several years ago, but I had put them in the shade and they went away.

Flower lovers are always eager to share plants, and I considered myself lucky to get away with only daisies. The plants were healthy and strong, and I immediately planted them, giving each division a generous dose of compost in its new home.

Susie is Susie Price Garrison. Susie and her husband Paul came to our wedding many years ago down in Cochran, Georgia, and when she saw we had used a daisy theme, Susie knew she and I would be friends. Our friendship has endured over the years and there have been many things in common other than our favorite flower and color.

So Susie offered me more daisy plants.

We found her working in her sunny plot set aside for flowers beside the big, white, two-story country home, and she was her usual charming, cheerful, generous self, offering far more plants than I could ever find space for.

Susie's daisies are the shastas with a row of white petals marching around a bright-yellow center. The stems are strong. Although good natured and easy to grow, the plant benefits from being divided when the clumps get large because, as with many other plants, the flowers get smaller as the group gets larger. They should be divided every two or three years.

Shastas require full sun, and although they will tolerate partial shade, the plants will not last as long nor the blooms be as prolific or as large. So if you have daisies, give them plenty of sun and put them in a rich humusy (aren't you beginning to wish you had made a compost heap?) soil, for they are heavy feeders. They also require plenty of water and good drainage.

They are most often used in borders or in beds where they can be cut without ruining the effect of the border. They make excellent cut flowers and are as much at home on a patio table as in a church arrangement.

Daisies should be divided in the spring. Plant them at the point where the stems meet the roots and they should be shaded a few days until new leaves appear, if possible. If you have trouble dividing an especially thick old clump, wash the soil away with a hose and you can see what you're doing.

The oldest daisy is the English daisy, a small 6-inch-high plant that comes in shades of rose, red, and white. Used as edging plants and in rock gardens, the plant reseeds so prolifically in the damp English climate that it can become a bother. It is frequently seen in English pastures and along the roadside, but here it does not behave that way. This semi-wild plant is *Bellis perennis* and is usually listed in the few catalogs that carry it as a biennial recommended for rock gardens and beds. There are several varieties ranging in height from 4 to 8 inches.

The word "daisy" comes from the Anglo-Saxon meaning "day's eye." Apparently the rays are supposed to be streaming from the sun, or center. The name "daisy" is today given to flowers of the family Compositae, alternatively called Asteraceae, and the chrysanthemum, arctotis, aster, rudbeckia, and townsendia all have similar characteristics. Although called a daisy, shastas are really members of the genus *Chrysanthemum* with the high-sounding name of *Chrysanthemum maximum*. In addition to the shasta, there is the oxeye, a wildflower that blooms in June. The arctic, nippon oxeye, and giant daisy are all white and bloom in September.

There is another popular daisy with the common name of painted lady. It is listed as Pyrethrum in catalogs. It may have either a single or double row of petals in white, rose, pink, or red shades. Another interesting note about this group of plants is that the dried flower heads are used to make insecticides and to make medicine for certain skin conditions.

Still another daisy grown in this area is the gloriosa daisy. Easy to grow and a good cut flower, it does well in borders or alone in beds. There are several varieties of the gloriosa, but all have bright-yellow petals with a green or brown center. The one exception is the bi-color daisy with some brown mixed in.

The Michaelmas daisy isn't really a daisy at all but another name for asters.

Shastas grow as perennials in our area, but there is another flower that has the daisy name that is an annual. The 20-inch Tahoka daisy or *Machaeranthera tanacetifolia* has fernlike foliage with blue petals around a yellow center. The daisy is often the choice of brides, and one florist complained bitterly to me last summer because she needed so many and none were available.

The daisy is almost always included in a list of favorite flowers, and it must have been a flower grower in love with spring and the sturdy, happy-looking white and yellow flower who first said, "fresh as a daisy."

Fourth Week
CHRYSANTHEMUMS

If I ever stop being a Jill-of-all-flowers and a master of one, that one will be the chrysanthemum. Although a perennial, it requires more care than the peony, iris, or day lily because it demands moving every year, or certainly every second year. It won't just die if you don't divide it, but as the clump gets more and more crowded, the individual plants will get more spindly and produce fewer blooms.

Chrysanthemums can be propagated in three ways: by seeds, which is best left to somebody else; by rooted cuttings; and by division of clumps in early spring. If you order plants you will probably get the second. If you already have a clump or if you have a generous neighbor, your new plants will come by way of the latter.

Chrysanthemums need sunshine. If planted in partial shade, they become spindly and bloom poorly. They are also sensitive to wind, so put them in a semi-protected place. This is true of many flowers that are harmed as much by wind as by shade and drought.

Chrysanthemums require a light, rich soil. Because they are heavy feeders, work well-rotted manure and about 2 or 3 inches of humus into the bed to a depth of 10 inches. In the absence of manure, spread 5–8–6 fertilizer around at the rate of 1 pound per 30 square feet.

Separate the plants from the old clump, throwing away the woody middle part. Work quickly so the roots won't dry. Place the small plants about 18 inches apart, setting them at the same or slightly below the level at which they were growing. Don't plant them too deep. Around each plant make a little saucerlike depression to hold the water and water them thoroughly. They will probably droop over and look pretty saggy, but in a day or so they'll be upright and on their way. If the plants have grown to more than 3 or 4 inches when you divide the clump, break

81

off about the top half to make up for root loss. This is the same as pruning bare root shrubs when you move them. In setting out small plants grown from cuttings in individual pots, plant them with the ball of soil and no topping is necessary because the roots are all intact. This "pruning" at transplanting time is different from pinching later for branch development.

Chrysanthemums have to have water. The hot summer days are their growing season, and if a lack of water causes a setback of growth, the bottom leaves get brown and withered, making the whole plant look bad. So regular watering is important, and give them a couple of more feedings if they look as if they need it.

There are two more points to successful chrysanthemum culture.

The first is pinching back. When the plants have three or four pairs of leaves, pinch out the top ½ inch, thus forcing the side branches to develop. When these branches grow to 6 inches, pinch off the tops. This will bring you into July, and if you want, you may give any new branches a third pinching, but don't do any pinching after the middle of July or you'll take the bud formation. This pinching makes the plant lower and bushier in growth with stronger stems that usually don't require staking, although there are some exceptions.

If the plant is fertilized, watered, and pinched, it will be strong, upright, and healthy looking instead of a limp, stringy thing that falls all over the ground.

The second thing to do is to keep the weeds away. Scratch about with your hoe for a week or two to catch any tiny weeds, then mulch the chrysanthemums with material from your compost pile to discourage other weed growth.

For the exhibitor interested in such things, there are 15 chrysanthemum classes with many varieties in each. Let us only note that there are more than 160 species in the genus *Chrysanthemum* and let it go at that. For us country gardeners it is sufficient to say that all chrysanthemums can be loosely divided into these categories: cushion, the low mounds covered with flowers often used for edging; pom pom, the small round flower; singles, those that look like daisies; decorative—these are the ones you get when you go to the hospital—large round flower with either incurved or reflex rays that is forced to its large size by disbudding; spoon, whose rays have little spoon shapes on the end; and the spider or quill mums that require more care than the others.

Another good point about chrysanthemums is the long blooming season that begins in August with the cushions and continues on until November or later, often defying frosts and outlasting most other flowers.

If you have a big, sunny place, a good idea is to plant your chrysanthemums in rows and then move them to the place you want them right before they bloom or even during blooming. Water them thoroughly the day before, then lift a large ball of soil with each plant. This way you can replace some annuals that have passed on. Next spring you can dig and separate the chrysanthemums and set them in rows again.

Not many plants would tolerate such treatment, and this tolerance makes them even more important to the gardener. It must be admitted that not every gardener wants to go to this much effort and chrysanthemums are usually planted where they are to bloom.

The exhibition business is another kettle of fish, but here we are talking about the gardener who wants some large blooms for home or church arrangements. To get these the home gardener uses another garden practice with chrysanthemums called disbudding. The singles don't benefit much from this, but the large decorative mums, including the incurve, reflex, and spider varieties, are all the better for it.

Always work from the top down so that if you accidentally knock off the top bud there will be flowers left below. Select the terminal bud on the tip top of the stem and remove any surrounding buds, going on down the stem removing any lateral growth and buds but do not remove any leaves. Don't do all this in one day. It is too much of a shock to the plant and it may lose too much sap. This way all the plant's nutrients will go to the one flower. You can follow a semi-disbudding practice by leaving the crown bud but removing those that encircle it and leaving the next two down the stem. Remove all others and the three flowers will be larger than usual but not so remarkable as the single flower would be.

You may have to stake the mums. It is desirable for the stems to be so healthy from all that fertilizer, sunshine, and water that they will be as sturdy as statues, but sometimes they get tall and the heavy flowers cause the plant to droop. Should this happen, put a stake in the center of the clump and loosely gather the center branches to it. Old stockings are good for tying up the branches. Don't tie up the whole clump, that looks worse than if it is falling on the ground.

Chrysanthemums can be used in many ways. They are often seen with other plants in a border, but I think they are much more spectacular when in a bed by themselves. Several clumps on each side of an entrance make a bright-colored spot. They are often used along walks and drives and are especially attractive in front of fences where their summer foliage is almost as pretty as the fall blooms.

The small cushion mums are often used as edgings, and it is these cushions, also, that find their way to window boxes and raised planters. Pots on porch and terrace almost cry to be filled with chrysanthemums. The cushions are normally used because of their low growth. Don't use the singles in pots as they are more spindly in growth and won't be as pretty.

To get a bigger show, if you are using decorative mums, use several cuttings or plants in one pot as the florists do. Cuttings can be taken now from the plants you neglected pinching. Instead of snipping out the top ½ inch, break off about 4 inches and put the cutting in sand or other potting medium and keep it damp and in good light but out of the sun. They should root in about three weeks. Start giving them sun to harden, then after a bit transplant to pots 7 to 10 inches in diameter.

If your porch or terrace is running over with geraniums, petunias, and other such, you can keep the pots someplace else until they are sporting blooming plants. Now that's what some folks would do. I would enjoy seeing the pot of greenery all summer, for I've never seen any place that had too many flowers or too much greenery. I think I should enjoy living in a jungle, save for the insects and the absence of an electric range.

Chrysanthemums make good cut flowers, but wait until they are open before cutting and don't take blooms from a wilted plant. The woody stems take up water slowly and they will probably continue to droop.

After they have bloomed, remove the flowers so they won't make seed. Some of them might survive and be nothing like their noble parents with the result that you'll have some strange looking flowers. In the South, you don't have to give them any special winter care, but your bed will look neater if you cut the stems back to 4 inches. If you don't, the chrysanthemums will come back next spring just as well.

Notes for May

June

First Week
GLADIOLI

You can't have a church flower arrangement or a wedding without gladioli. You could just as easily get along without a groom.

Most all gardeners plant a few glads and they are special favorites of men gardeners. The one thing that bothers me about the way people plant glads is planting a dozen bulbs in a straight row along the front of the house or edge of the yard. They look like flowering fence posts.

There are two ways to properly locate them.

If you want a few for cut flowers or just for looking, put them in your border with other plants in clusters of at least six. This way you have a bright patch of color. The tall, upright growth also provides a rather dashing accent in a border of low- to medium-height plants.

The second way is for the serious grower. He plants them in rows in the cutting garden. When done this way you'll probably get larger blooms because they are easier to care for. Commercial growers follow this method, and if you are the unofficial supplier of flowers for your church or community, you might want to do them this way also. But please, please don't plant a straight row of single plants around your house or on the side of the yard.

The late Mr. and Mrs. Joe Douthit grew glads commercially on their farm near Pendleton, S.C., for many years and area people remember their beautiful flowers. Mrs. Douthit said her husband always planted bulbs every two weeks from late spring through August to get continuous bloom until frost. Following their excellent example you still have plenty of time to plant glads. Some varieties bloom in 60 days and others take as long as 150 days to produce their flowers.

From the standard varieties that will grow to five feet down to the miniatures there are sizes and beautiful colors that were not available some years ago.

Another thing Mr. Douthit did that the home gardener can imitate was to buy medium-sized bulbs. Growing commercially as he did, he bought bulbs by the bushel, and he contended that the medium-sized bulbs produced flower spikes almost as splendid as the larger bulbs and were much less expensive.

In planting gladiolus corms, either in beds or in rows, set them about 4 to 6 inches deep. Because of their upright growth they can be placed as close together as 4 inches. If planted in rows, leave about 18 inches between rows so you can get in there to work among them.

The gladiolus is another one of those flowers that is a good choice for the beginning gardener because it doesn't make great demands on either the gardener or the soil. It will survive a considerable amount of neglect, but like a child or a dairy cow, it produces more with good care.

The soil should be fairly loose and humusy. If you use manure, be sure it is well composted or you may get certain diseases in the corms. Wood ashes and bone meal are both good natural soil builders and a complete commercial fertilizer such as 4–12–12 can be used or superphosphate substituted. The best way to use all fertilizers and soil additives is to dig them into the bottom of your trench, cover with an inch of soil, then place the corms on top. When the leaf spikes get some size, mulch the plants with whatever is available to keep down weeds and keep in moisture.

Glads need a lot of water. If the weather is dry, you can run the sprinkler all night to be sure the ground is soaked. Some authorities say the soil around them should be slightly damp at all times.

The best time to cut glads is either in early morning or late afternoon. Try not to cut any leaves with the spikes because the leaves are needed to manufacture food for the bulb. Using a sharp knife, cut on a long slant so the stem can take up more water. Some people like to wait until the first two pair of florets are open, but the spikes will last longer if you cut them as soon as the two bottom florets are showing color.

In our area, most glad corms will safely winter in the ground if they are set 6 inches deep. Some may require lifting, and if so, wait until after the first frost then pull or dig them up and cut off the tops. Store the corms in a cool place, but be sure the "cool" is not so cool that they freeze. You may as well leave them in the ground if you do that. If mice are a problem, get yourself a cat and also put a few moth balls in the box with the bulbs.

Gladioli make a beautiful display in the garden, but I think their greatest value is as cut flowers. They last a long time, come in many colors, and their shape provides the height often needed in arrangements. They are of easy culture. The corms are relatively inexpensive and usually last several years.

What else should you expect from a flower?

Second Week
HANGING BASKETS

The whole thing may go back to King Nebuchadnezzar of Babylon who, in order to keep his mountain bride from being homesick, constructed terraces atop his palace, filling them with trees, shrubs, and flowers. We don't know if his bride was happier, but his efforts with the hanging gardens made them counted among the Seven Wonders of the Ancient World.

Homesick brides and ancient wonders aside, hanging plant containers are enjoyed more and more by the average gardener. They are at home indoors if they get the necessary light, but are especially attractive on porches and terraces. The top rule with them is to keep them out of the line of traffic or to have them suspended high enough not to give a guest an unexpected bang on the head.

Hanging baskets can be hung from ceilings, beams, limbs, overhead trellises, eaves, and other places. There are hooks that screw into the beams to hold them. These should be sturdy because a newly watered basket can be quite heavy, and if the whole thing comes splattering down, imagine what a mess it will be to clean—not to mention the damage to the plant.

Several kinds of baskets are available. The most commonly used and least expensive is the wire one for which you buy a liner. These can also be lined with sheet sphagnum moss, then filled with a mixture of good soil, sand, and humus to hold the plants. One fellow says you can line the wire basket with black plastic film with just as good and sometimes better results. First line it, put in the soil, then cut the excess plastic from the edges. These don't look quite as good as the moss-lined ones, but they are easier, cheaper, don't leak, and don't dry out as quickly. If you use enough trailing vines the black plastic will be mostly covered.

You can also buy holders that fit standard clay pots so that plants already growing well can be air-borne. At one time when everyone was in the macramé craze all kinds of clay and ceramic containers were being held aloft by ropes with clever little knots. I was never into knots. These are not seen much now but they were effective hangers.

There are wooden tubs, wooden slat baskets, and plastic containers available at garden stores. If you are one of those clever persons who can look at a brick and think of 17 artistic things to do with it (the only thing I can think to do with a brick is to use it for a doorstop), you can come up with containers from kettles, gourds, ceramic pots, and all kinds of unlikely items. Do provide drainage, either through holes in the bottom or by placing gravel in the container before adding the soil. If you have the time, talent, or interest you can fashion your own wire baskets from metal clothes hangers. I don't plan to do that anytime soon.

For those not quite so ingenious most greenhouses, garden shops and even supermarkets offer already planted pots. You simply go home, get a hook, chain, and nail and hang them. Sometimes these are planted with selections that I don't really think are best for hanging baskets. Other greenhouse folk will plant them for you if you tell them the colors or flowers you want. But it's really such fun to arrange the basket and watch it grow that I should think you would rather do it yourself.

In planting a hanging basket, always put the plants close together to give a running-over look. If you stick in a few little plants thinking they will grow and fill it, several weeks will be gone before the basket is attractive. I prefer to use at least two kinds of plants, and more would be better. Put something tall in the center and shorter plants around the outside, interspersed with a plant that trails downward such as ivy, periwinkle, trailing geranium, wandering Jew, etc. If only one plant is chosen, such as a fern, be sure you put in enough plants for the basket to look filled to running over.

You can use all foliage plants, but I like blooming plants in the house or on the porch if they can get the exposure they need. There are some plants, such as cascading petunias and trailing geraniums that are especially suitable for the hanging containers.

There are two ways of watering a hanging basket.

The first, recommended by folks who are supposed to know, is by putting the whole thing in a tub of slightly warm water until the sphagnum moss liner and inside soil absorb all the water they will hold, then putting it someplace until the dripping stops. You wait until it is dry to the touch before repeating the episode. Can you imagine what a mess that would make in the kitchen?

Then there is my way. I just take a quart canning jar and pour warm water into the thing. When that is absorbed, I pour in a little more. Hanging baskets may require watering every day or so in hot, dry weather because they are constantly losing water through evaporation on all sides. If you aren't going to keep them watered, then don't bother with them at all.

The same exposure considerations must be used for selecting plants for baskets as for any other space. If your hanging container is in the shade, you might consider planting it with shrimp plants, both tuberous and fibrous begonias, campanulas, coleuses, English ivies, wax plants, monkey flowers, peppermints, geraniums, strawberry geraniums, wandering Jews, ferns, and others.

Baskets receiving full sun would look good filled with verbenas, dianthus, petunias, trailing lantanas, portulacas, nasturtiums, Cape marigolds, cushion mums, fuchias, and other sun lovers.

Flowers in hanging containers, as do most flowers, benefit from frequent and light applications of liquid fertilizer, as well as a mulch.

A lavishly filled and blooming hanging basket can change an ordinary spot into a special one.

Third Week
AGERATUMS

When my neighbor Mrs. Willard Bishop gave me several plants of hardy ageratums many years ago, she told me not to put them around the front of the house. Being younger, skinnier, and more ignorant of flower culture than now, I did so anyway.

I pulled ageratum for years after that, and was still giving it away until I moved across the road and left it.

It was cut down, pulled up, pushed over, stepped on, and had harsh words directed toward it, but each spring it came up again. I gave it to kin, friend, and total strangers. The cosmetic lady, Bible salesman, or passerby asking directions could not escape until each had a generous handful of hardy ageratums wrapped in damp newspaper.

Now I am not opposed to ageratum. I acknowledge it to be a lovely, useful flower. I just wish it had not been so persistent in its growth among the foundation shrubs. As the ageratum spread, my friendship with Mrs. Bishop cooled.

There are two kinds of ageratums. The annual, sometimes called floss flower, found as bedding plants in garden stores in spring, is the one most commonly grown. It varies in height from a tiny 2- to 3-inch compact plant to 18 inches, and it is a favorite edging plant.

If you have luck with starting seeds indoors, you can propagate it yourself. You can wait until it is warm and plant it outdoors, but then it is so late blooming that the earlier start is better. The best thing to do is to buy plants from a greenhouse where they have the proper conditions for getting the plants off to a good start.

Ageratum is one of the annuals that resows itself, and the flower can soon become established in your garden with plants to transplant or share the following spring. It can also be propagated by cuttings in the spring. Any transplanting should be done early when the plant is very small. Ageratums prefer full sun but will do fairly well in light shade.

The best-known variety is the Blue Mink, the 6-inch little blue beauty so often used in edgings. There are other varieties such as Blue Blazer and Blue Danube whose shades of blue and bluish-lavender and differences in height make them desirable for the border or bed in your garden. There is also a dwarf white variety that combines well with a colorful, slightly taller plant.

The flowering heads should be removed when they die. This will extend the season of bloom until frost. The official name of this annual plant is *Ageratum houstonianum*.

Then there is my friend that has overrun everything. It is really not ageratum at all but a plant named *Eupatorium coelestinum* and sometimes called mistflower, but more often incorrectly called perennial ageratum. Its flowers are more violet than blue; it reaches 3 feet in height; and it doesn't begin blooming until September. This is the plant you usually see at fairs listed as ageratum. The leaf texture and formation and flowers are very similar to the small annual so the mistflower's adopted, though incorrect, name is understandable.

Because of their bunchy growth, you can pretty well leave the dwarf annuals alone except for removing the spent blossoms, but the larger annuals and the perennial both benefit from pinching. This means breaking off the top ½ inch of the plant to force the side branches to grow. The perennial almost demands it or it will grow very tall and scraggly.

Although the uses of both the annual and the perennial are many, the perennial ageratum's best use seems to be to fill a sunny corner where it can be left alone and spread to its heart's content. It benefits from being lifted and reset every couple of years, but you get just about as good results and a lot less muscle strain by pulling plants from the center of the mass to give to folks who happen your way.

The primary reasons I object to them in the front border is that their growth is too tall for the shrubs, and their stalks are unattractive after the first frost. If you put them someplace where you won't have to work around them all the time, they will more than pay for their space by providing you with attractive foliage in the spring and summer and fluffy lavender blooms in the fall.

The tiny annual ageratum is often shown as an edging plant in front of dwarf yellow marigolds, but it is equally as pretty in front of white or pink petunias. The annual can be used in window boxes, planters, and rock gardens, and because of its compact growth and unusual blue color, it is attractive in pots for porch and patio.

Many people find ageratum's color its best feature. Because of the limited number of blue flowers, it does have real value in adding sparkle to a border usually dominated by reds, pinks, whites, and yellows.

Use ageratum, but don't put the perennial beside your front door. Mrs. Bishop said not to.

Fourth Week
HYDRANGEAS

"I want you and Ed to come see my hydrangeas."

I can still remember the invitation from the late Mrs. Elmina Smith, our neighbor whose husband was the founder of Smith's water-ground corn meal. I remember also the gigantic water-wheel that turned his mill until that particular county landmark was captured by the waters of Hartwell Lake.

So on a Sunday afternoon I moseyed over for a look and caught her talking up a storm with her sister, Mrs. Annie Garrison, who was there for a visit. Miss Elmina and sister Annie were part of the Mayes family of Townville, S.C., and have always shared an interest in flowers, although early domestic chores kept them from the flower garden when they were young girls.

Mrs. Smith had three hydrangea bushes. On the largest bush, measuring 6 feet across and 4 feet high, I counted more than a hundred blooms. She said I could double the number because the blunt stems gave evidence of many cut blooms. Two of the plants bore light-blue flowers, but the largest had the deep, vivid blue so desired in a hydrangea. She told me what she did. The plant, in a small bucket, had been a gift from Annie right before she moved from her former home north of Walhalla, S.C. Mrs. Smith had planted it in ordinary soil but

97

had dug the hole deep and wide so the gentle roots could grow. Each spring she worked rotted manure into the soil around the shrub.

It would seem that the first thing a fellow must do to have picture-book flowers is to buy a cow.

There are several kinds of hydrangeas.

The one seen most in this Piedmont area is the big-leaf French hydrangea, or *Hydrangea macrophylla*. Some plants have pink flowers, others blue, but the color of both can be changed by altering the pH of the soil. A blue flower requires a soil pH of 5.5 or under. To make the same flower pink, the soil can be made alkaline to a pH reading of 6.7 or over with the addition of lime. Some shrubs, obviously confused and planted in wishy-washy soil, produce pink and blue flowers on the same plant. Sometimes both shades appear on the same bloom. This results from a soil that is between 6.7 and 7.2 on the pH scale.

If your plant is in moderately acid soil and producing light-blue flowers, add aluminum sulphate to get the dark-blue color. It is not really the acidity of the soil that does it; it is the aluminum in the soil that makes the flower blue, but the soil must be acid or the aluminum cannot be used by the plant. So, you see, you need both. Aluminum sulphate is available at most garden stores but common alum (potassium alum) can be used instead.

Plant new hydrangeas in the fall or early spring. Mix in some rotted manure or humus from your compost heap and then add the aluminum sulphate using about ½ pound for each bushel of soil.

You cannot change the color of all hydrangeas, only the *Hydrangea machrophylla*.

The peegee hydrangea, *Hydrangea paniculata grandiflora*, has a cone-shaped bloom beginning in August and lasting until frost. The blooms begin white, turn to a light pink, then change to buff. This variety can take more cold than the French ones and is the plant grown by our northern neighbors.

Hydrangea anomala petiolaris is a climbing hydrangea that can also live in the colder climates and produces white flowers in July. It starts slowly but will reach 40 feet or more if you leave it alone and give it something to climb on. The color of neither the peegee nor the climber will be affected by the aluminum treatment.

Most hydrangea varieties prefer an exposure of part sun/part filtered shade. They wilt quickly in full, hot sun and if they are in full shade they don't flower well.

The reason some hydrangeas don't bloom is that the buds have been killed by cold or chopped off by an eager pruner. Like most flowering shrubs, the hydrangea sets about forming buds for the following summer in the early fall, so if you prune it in the late fall or spring, you take the buds. If you think you have to prune to maintain a desired size or shape, do it immediately after the plant finishes blooming. Some plants bloom on last year's growth, some on the current spring's. In the case of the former, a severe pruning would sacrifice a year's blooms, so you have to know which plant you have.

Because the buds are already set, they are sometimes killed if left unprotected in the colder regions of the South. An easy way, and the way I almost always prefer, is to cover them with leaves, working the leaves down between the branches.

Hydrangeas require lots of water and are one of the first shrubs to show droopy leaves in its absence. Miss Annie said a sprinkler is the thing to use so that the leaves also get a good wetting, but watering the roots would probably do just as well.

If you receive a hydrangea pot plant as a gift transplant it to your garden in the fall or spring and its growth will surprise you.

Hydrangeas can be used in many places in the garden, but I prefer not to use them as foundation plants because, for all their good qualities, such as beautiful foliage, lovely and brilliant blooms, and easy maintenance, they do have the disadvantage of dropping their leaves and looking like a bunch of sticks in winter—not the best thing beside your front door.

The hydrangea can get to be a sizable plant, but if you have the space and proper exposure, one will be an asset to your yard.

Notes for June

July

First Week
CANNAS

I want to say several words in the defense of cannas. Some horticultural snobs consider them fit only for decorating water-filtering plants and cemeteries, but I think they have suffered from bad public relations.

The canna does about all you can expect a plant to do. It produces bright blooms above attractive foliage, it is easy to get started, and it requires only minimal care. If someone wants a plant to fuss over, let him get orchids, but if he wants dependability year after year, he should try cannas.

This very dependability is responsible for their great use around public buildings where maximum effect with minimum effort is desired.

I have several cannas, and each year I put out others, for I have a love for the canna that is shared by many other folk in our Southland. One such person is Mrs. Estelle Glenn, a city neighbor whose drive on one side was lined with many plants in shades of red, pink, and yellow until she changed the planting a few years ago.

The usual way to start cannas is with a tuber from the garden shop or from a division of an old clump. This dividing should be done every three or four years or the clump becomes too crowded. With a sharp knife, assuming you can find such a thing in your house, cut the tubers so that there is an eye on each one.

Cannas may be planted in early spring in ordinary garden soil, which doesn't mean clay or sand, and as with other summer bulbs, should be fertilized at the time of planting. Cover the tubers with 2 inches of soil.

If you mixed compost into the planting soil, more fertilizing will not be needed the first year, but after that you had better feed them because such large plants are pretty heavy feeders.

Some growers work well-rotted manure around each plant in the early spring then as the growth comes along, each one is given a sprinkling, maybe a couple of teaspoonfuls, of 5-10-10 commercial fertilizer. Now our organic gardeners would much rather use some of the humus from their compost heaps, first mixed into the soil at planting time, then as a mulch around the plants when growth begins.

If you want to try it, cannas can be started from seed, but because of their hardness, soak them in water at least a day before planting them directly where you want them or in peat pots for moving outside later.

Give cannas full sun or almost that.

The plants have already started blooming here in July and will continue off and on until frost with clusters of blooms forming as others fade. Once seen only in the bright-red variety, President, the flower is now available in shades of yellow, salmon, rosy pink, coral, primrose, creamy white, and many variegated combinations.

The giant or standard plant grows to a height of between 3 and 4 feet and sometimes more, depending on the variety and care. Such height and the luxuriant foliage make it most desirable as a background plant in a perennial border. Their height, color, and foliage also make them good accent plants at the end of a low border, the corner of the house, in a clump at the end of the drive, or in any other such place where an eyecatcher is needed.

The canna is also excellent for that sunny corner that you want to fill with something that won't demand your poking around it all the time. The plant is also economical. One canna quickly fills a space that would require many smaller, and possibly more expensive plants. The bright foliage gives a tropical atmosphere to a patio from early summer until frost. Daughter Gaye says ours looks like a jungle. Mrs. Glenn had cannas growing inside around the edge of her sun porch or garden room and said that sometimes she has blooms at Christmas time.

The dwarf varieties make good pot plants for a sunny porch, deck, or patio. If you used them inside in a sunroom it would have to be a large room for the proportion of such a large plant to be pleasing.

These dwarf varieties grow to about two and a half feet and can be used with shrubbery in borders, or in front of the giant varieties in a canna bed. This all-canna bed is one of the best ways to use the plant if you have enough sunny space.

Cannas do have to have water. Like dahlias and other tuberous rooted plants, their soil must be well drained, but the plant should be watered frequently during dry weather.

Another one of the good things about living in the South is that cannas can stay in the ground over winter. Our northern neighbors have to dig them in the fall after frost has killed the leaves and store them until next spring. That seems a lot of bother, so I think I'll just stay here south of the Mason-Dixon where I belong.

Second Week
BIENNIALS

When you see from your kitchen window the healthy row of petunias with their fluffy blooms, the dwarf marigolds standing up straight—as if they were trying to be taller—the daisies, snapdragons, zinnias and other things that fill your yard with color and love, aren't you glad you got up and did something this spring instead of sitting around watching the make-believe adventures of soap-opera heroines?

Your garden is at its peak, and you have relaxed enjoying the flowers as they grow and those you bring into the house, spending your time only in the pleasant task of maintenance.

Your fingernails are halfway back in shape, and you may think all that digging and scratching are over, but they aren't. A garden is never finished, and there are two jobs that must be done in July if you haven't done them already. The first is moving irises, but that is another story, and the second is planting biennial seeds.

Biennials are often overlooked by gardeners, or at least by the more impatient of the breed. They like to plant a marigold seed today and have it bloom in six weeks. They have little truck for something that won't bloom for another year. There are times when gardeners must practice the patience of Job. Think of the fellow who plants a century plant.

Biennials are defined as those plants that require a full year to complete their cycle. They are planted one summer, transplanted into their permanent location in the fall or following spring, bloom in the summer, and die. Then you start over again with more seed.

This isn't as involved as it seems. In fact, it is a real advantage because you aren't too busy in the yard right now, and if you transplant the little fellows in the fall, they'll be getting ready to bloom next spring or summer without your worrying too much more about them. With all the work there is to be done in the spring, I should think you would be grateful for something you can plant now instead of complaining about it.

Some of these biennials turn out to be perennials. Some varieties just do that, so don't worry about which one will or won't. Some of these biennials reseed themselves and give the impression of being perennials but they aren't. If you are in there every day with the hoe going chop-chop-chop, you'll keep the seed all bothered and then kill any that may survive and sprout.

I have one example of this, the *Cleome soineosa,* or spider flower. It is an annual, but the last two springs little plants have popped up all over the place from seed the plant dropped the summer before.

Some of the prettiest flowers are biennials. They can be planted from June to August, but July seems to be the best month.

First, select your seedbed. Make it of good soil, finely pulverized. You may even want to shake it through a ¼-inch screen. Plant the seed and keep the seedbed damp. This should be in a shady or partially shaded spot because not many little seedlings can survive the hot summer sun.

Second, when the seedlings have put out three or four sets of leaves, you should transplant them. You can do this two ways. If the plants are crowded, simply move them to another spot giving them plenty of growing room. If you have sown the seed thinly, they may be able to stay where they are by removing some of the crowding plants but that is doubtful.

Third, in the fall move them to where you want them to bloom in your perennial border or wherever. You may wait and move them early next spring. It is a good idea to mulch them over the winter. One exception is the hollyhock, which should be transplanted in the fall simply because it's easier on your back. The hollyhock has a long taproot that should always be planted straight down, so unless you want to dig a hole in which you could plant a telephone pole next spring, you had best move them in the fall before they get very large.

Most folks run out and buy expensive pansy plants in the winter or early spring when they could easily grow their own by planting them August. It's also more fun, not to mention the economy.

In addition to pansies and hollyhocks, sweet william is another favorite plant that should be sown now for bloom next spring. It is another one that reseeds itself prolifically, so once you get it started, it will be with you for years if you don't chop up the seedlings.

Speaking of reseeding, I recall a visit with Mr. and Mrs. Hollister Moore in their beautiful lake home near Seneca, S.C. She showed me her snapdragons. She had bought plants the year before that produced lovely flowers, but was surprised this spring to see the plants up in March and blooming in May. She said the blooms were much lovelier this year and the plants had healthier stems with longer spikes of blooms. This was another example of reseeding.

Foxglove, or digitalis, is a valuable biennial sending up tall spires of pink, white, purple, and rose in June and July. Some of these turn out to be perennials, but plant them now. Forget-me-nots or myosotis, English daisies, Iceland poppies, Canterbury bells, wallflowers, honesty plants, and others fall into this group of biennials.

Second Week
FALL VEGETABLES

Planting anything with the word cold in it during the hot days of July is a comforting thought. There are "cole" crops and "cold" crops.

The word "cole" means members of the genus *Brassica* or the mustard family and includes several kinds of vegetables that do require cool weather. There are other "cold"-weather vegetables that produce best during cool days. Some of these are often planted in early spring in the Piedmont and many do well but others bolt or die as soon as the days warm thereby decreasing their productivity.

Both the "cole" crops and the cold-weather crops are best planted in mid-July or later so that they will mature just as the calendar approaches frosty nights. Some of the plants such as collards and parsnips need the frost to sweeten the taste. Many of these vegetables will take really low temperatures and sometimes last through the whole winter.

These cool-weather vegetables usually follow the earlier veggies in successive plantings to get two crops off the same space during the year. An example is the Brussels sprout, *Brassica aleracea gemmifera*. After the green bush beans are harvested in July, sow the Brussels sprout seeds to get plants which you will transplant into rows in mid-August.

Collards, *Brassica aleracea acephula*, take 60 to 80 days to maturity, depending on the variety, from seeds sown in August. Sow the seeds sparsely then thin the seedlings leaving the main crop in place or make a seedbed and transplant the seedlings to a row. The plants get large and need 18 to 24 inches between plants. Collards are extremely high in vitamins A, B, and C and are an excellent source of iron.

Broccoli, *Brassica oleracea italica*, should also be planted in July with the seedlings either thinned or transplanted to stand about 20 inches apart in the row.

Rutabagas which require about three months to maturity can be planted in July or early August. They are sometimes called yellow turnips and are planted for the large root. This root, a good source of vitamins A and C and calcium, is harvested when it is about the size of a baseball. Those in stores are usually larger than they should be for best flavor.

Carrots, planted by most gardeners in very early spring, are also a good fall crop. They need 60 to 75 days to maturity and should be planted in late July or early August. Parsnips need longer to mature, about 100 days. They should be planted in mid-summer and need the early frosts to sweeten the flavor. They can be left in the garden all winter: no freezing, canning, storing or drying. This parsnip is too often overlooked by Piedmont gardeners. It's a good source of potassium.

Mid to late summer is also the time to make a second planting of garden peas. They require 50 to 73 days to maturity so count your days in order that they will mature before the first frost in your area. They will take the first light frosts if mature but the heavy killing frosts will get them. If you have planted garden peas only in the early spring you will be pleasantly surprised to find that these fall-planted ones are even better than the delicious spring ones.

When early August arrives plant cauliflower seeds outdoors to get transplants. Cauliflower, *Brassica aleracea botrytis*, can go into the frosty nights also.

At the same time plant turnips and mustard. Mustard is ready to eat almost before you can get back into the house requiring only 20 to 50 days. Turnips need 35 to 70 days. Some gardeners broadcast these but I prefer planting them in rows.

A little later when early fall arrives plant spinach. It needs from 40 to 70 days to mature again because of the different varieties. It also withstands frosts.

In August and September plant Chinese cabbage, *Brassica pekinensis*, which needs two months to the eating stage. About the same time plant kale, 35 to 60 days, and sow seeds of cabbages in time for transplants to be set in rows around September 1. There are many varieties of cabbages, *Brassica aleracea capitata*, with widely differing maturing times.

In late summer and into September make several plantings of lettuce. Despite its fragile appearance lettuce is a tough little plant and will take temperatures down to the mid 20s if they have a light mulch such as straw or leaves. Plantings of radishes can be made in late September and on into October. One of the quickest vegetables to mature, some varieties are ready for harvest in 25 days but others take about twice that. Radishes should be planted to mature before frost.

Third Week
NASTURTIUMS

One year I had pumpkins in my planter.

I didn't plan to have pumpkins sprawling all over the entrance and half the front yard, making every effort to get into the living room in one direction and into the highway in the other. It just happened.

The year before, my neighbor the late Pete Cooper and I were partners in a pumpkin venture that produced more pumpkins that anybody needed. Some of them died on us, and with out any departing rites we dumped them onto the compost heap.

The following spring I added a couple of wheelbarrows full of this humus to the planter. Although most seed are killed by the heat within the compost pile, the pumpkin seed proved very durable, and in a few days here came the pumpkin plants. I pulled up most of them, for I had planned petunias and geraniums for the planter that year—not pumpkins. At the middle of summer there were still two plants that had filled the planter, spilled over the edge onto the ground, producing a rather attractive, and most healthy vine with large yellow blooms and even some pumpkins. But as soon as a few of the pumpkins matured, I pulled up that vine. The following year I planned for nasturtiums.

It's surprising how rarely nasturtiums pop up in casual conversation. Maybe like spouses and electricity they are taken for granted.

The beginning gardener should meet nasturtiums early in his gardening career. In his novitiate he should select only those plants that grow easily and successfully so that he can be proud of himself and have the enthusiasm to go on to more difficult gardening endeavors.

Nasturtiums would go on any easy-to-grow list. They are annuals. You sow them in the spring, they bloom, and die in one year. They make few demands. They grow well in average-to-poor garden soil, even that which is sandy or gravelly. Too rich soil makes them produce more foliage than flowers, as it does with marigolds. They do have to be in full sun.

Prepare the bed where they are to bloom by digging the soil a spade's depth, and you can work in some humus if you like. Plant the seed, covering them with 1 inch of soil. Nasturtiums germinate in about 8 days and when they are a couple of inches high or less, you should thin them to about a foot apart. They will start blooming about a month after planting and continue until frost gets them.

Of the almost 50 varieties of nasturtiums, the one most commonly grown is the dwarf double, *Tropaeolum minor,* that grows about a foot high with a 1½-foot spread. They flower very freely and the blooms are in shades of red, yellow, orange, salmon, and creamy white. This dwarf plant is very good for edgings, walks and borders. It can be used in planters (usually preferred to pumpkins), window boxes, and pots for porch or patio.

There is a tall nasturtium, *Tropaeolum majus,* that reaches 3 or 4 feet and can be trained on strings and trellises. They are double or semi-double.

The old-fashioned single nasturtium grows about 1½-feet high and blooms so prolifically that it is very good for cutflowers.

There is also a climbing nasturtium, the canarybird vine, *Tropaeolum peregrinum,* that grows from 8 to 12 feet high and is especially suitable for training on columns, fences, and mailbox posts.

The single or double small plants are very good for hanging baskets in the sun. They can be used alone, quickly filling the basket and tumbling over the side, or you can use a taller, upright plant in the center with the nasturtiums around the outer edge.

Nasturtiums make good cut flowers, lasting several days in arrangements or in a bowl by themselves. Nasturtiums can also be used for drying. Some people are fond of the sunny little plant for its pleasant fragrance.

Both the flowers and young tender leaves are useful in cooking. Use them in sandwiches and salads as you would lettuce. The seeds of the old-fashioned single varieties are also used for salads and pickles. The newer dwarf doubles don't produce as many seeds.

Nasturtiums also make a colorful show inside during the winter when their bright blossoms are a welcome addition to the usual collection of foliage plants. You have to have a sunny window. Plant several seeds in a 4- or 5-inch pot, removing all but the strongest when they come up. As the plant grows, train it on a string attached to the curtain rod or something. Give it water, and you should have nasturtium blooms all winter. These can be started most anytime, but unless sun comes in your window most of the day, don't start it at all.

If you haven't grown nasturtiums, plan now to add this cheerful, easy-to-grow plant to your garden.

Fourth Week
RED-HOT POKERS

Gardening is much like woman's work: it's never done. Just when you think you've got things in order, you discover there is something else that needs attention.

Several years ago our little Lee, then in elementary school, while visiting a playmate overheard a woman visitor in the home saying that when she got up each morning she didn't know what to do all day. Lee came home and perkily suggested the lady ought to plant a garden!

That was good advice from the mouth of a babe, because either a flower or vegetable garden would have kept the good lady busy as many hours a day as she chose. Even here in summer when the garden is a showplace of blooms, there is work to be done for next season.

One such job is planting perennials, which is very much like the cultivation of biennials, but there is one perennial that takes a bit more work. It is tritoma, commonly called torch lily, red-hot poker, or flame flower, although its real name is *Kniphofia uvaria,* and it is of the family Liliaceae, the lily family.

Knowing very little about the plant except to admire it, I consulted Mrs. Bill Johnston of our town who was well known locally for her beautiful yard and her garden club work.

She had some established clumps in the brilliant red color and some newer groups that she started from seed. She

115

generously shared with me her experience with the plant, and after her enthusiastic recommendation, I should think the whole world would rush out and plant tritomas.

To begin with, tritoma is a perennial, and a sturdy one at that. It is also one of the flowers most often recommended for a perennial border by folks who are supposed to know what they're talking about.

Here in the South it lives year after year, coming up again each spring without being disturbed. Our northern neighbors, poor things, have to take it up each winter, transplanting it to a cold frame until spring, then reset it. Now I know for sure and certain I would never do all that.

Torch lily is a large plant. It has coarse, grasslike leaves with a bloom spike that sometimes reaches 3 or 4 feet. The bloom cluster starts opening at the bottom like a gladiolus, and as the blooms age, they grow lighter in color. Tops of the newly opened blooms are a bright color, so the blossom spike gives a two-toned, or torch, appearance. At the beginning of the blooming period in mid-June, the hollow bloom stalks are erect, but as the flower heads get heavier and heavier, the stalks lean and curve about, a characteristic that can be used to advantage by an artistic flower arranger.

The plant's size puts it at the rear of the border, and Mrs. Johnston suggested setting them in groups of ten or twelve, each plant about 1½ or 2 feet from its neighbor. The plant does multiply, so by giving it this much growing room it won't have to be reset for several years.

Her plants were in full sun, but she had a neighbor whose plants received only afternoon sun and did well. It might be a good practice for the beginning gardener to plan a sunny exposure.

They require a lot of water. It was Mrs. Johnston's contention that if a plant has plenty of water and fertilizer it can withstand a lot of other neglect and abuse. She said her husband accused her of watering plants even during a rain. The development of anything, whether children, chickens, or chinaberries, depends on the care it gets, and to get a super red-hot poker plant you have to give it plenty of water.

New plants may be obtained by separating an existing clump in early spring when the new growth first starts, Mrs. Johnston said. Don't wait until the growth is large or the plant will resent being bothered. A new plant will probably bloom that first summer, or if it doesn't, it will the second. Water tritomas well to get them established.

She also had some plants she started from seed and now is the time to begin such a project. These tiny seed should be sown in July or August. She used flats filled with a special seed-bed mixture of vermiculite she bought at the seed store. She kept the soil damp until the little sprouts appeared and said there were so many of them that each seed must have come up twice!

From time to time she fed them with a water-soluble fertilizer, kept them watered, and left them undisturbed in the flats outdoors all winter. The following spring she took little clumps of them and put them in the ground. They were so tightly packed that it was difficult to separate them. They grew a year in this new home until the following spring when she took them up, separated them, and planted them in the permanent location. They bloomed a few months later that summer.

This may seem like a lot of trouble, but it isn't if you like flowers. During this year and a half she was doing other things not just standing there looking at them grow. The plants are expensive if purchased, so you see the wisdom of planting seeds.

The soil into which she put the plants was rich in humus. She laughingly said half her yard was sand and the other half clay, and over the years she had constantly worked to improve both sides by adding sawdust, rotted manure, and more recently, ground leaves. All this humus-making material had been worked into the area she chose for the permanent location of the red-hot poker.

In addition to her frequent waterings, she used the instant-type water-soluble fertilizer whenever she could get to it or whenever the plants looked as if they needed it.

Tritomas are most often seen in the bright, orangey-red, but shades of coral-red, white, and yellow are also available.

Red-hot poker makes an excellent cut flower. It lasts a week or more indoors with the addition of fresh water each day and combines well with other yellow and orange flowers.

Granted that getting plants established from seed may require some effort, but once started either from seed or divisions, the tritoma is one of the easiest perennials because it doesn't need the pinching, staking, dividing, or protecting that some of the other perennials do.

The bright blooms in June and July are a real eyecatcher in the garden or indoors and you should try to make a place for it in your planting.

Notes for July

August

First Week
CRAPE MYRTLES

At this time each year here in our beautiful South you are probably awed, as I am, by the beauty of the crape myrtles in full bloom. If you do not have crape myrtles in your yard, please consider adding at least one.

Crape myrtles are quite easy to grow in our part of the country. Our northern friends have a problem with them. They have to give them careful winter protection and the tops still die to the ground. Often even the roots don't survive. They are usually treated as a tub plant, and even if used in the yard, they never become the crimson-tipped trees that they do here. Northern gardeners have a better climate than we do for delphiniums and lupines so Mama Nature is fair.

Here, however, the crape myrtle grows and blooms quite easily as long as you give them their few requirements.

Several years ago one leading farm magazine pushed the crape myrtle for rural beautification, suggesting it be used to line highways and property lines. Many cities use this tree for beautifying their streets.

The crape myrtle can be kept as a bush, used as a tub plant for the patio, brought inside in a pot, or allowed to grow into a tree that will reach 15 or 20 feet. There are not many plants that grow so easily and lend themselves to such varied treatment.

The crape myrtle's formal name is *Lagerstroemia indica*, of the family Myrtaceae. It is a "first cousin" to the bog myrtle, sand myrtle, and creeping myrtle, also known as *Vinca minor*, or periwinkle. Although the 20-foot crape myrtle tree and the little ground-cover periwinkle are different in size, a close examination of the leaf formation will show a similarity.

Although available in white, lavender and several shades of pink, the rosy-red crape myrtle that used to be known as Watermelon is my favorite. I don't see it listed in catalogs now.

Not only have the plant people developed new colors and names but they also have given us the dwarf, 3-foot plant and 7-foot semi-dwarf trees.

About the only demand crape myrtle really makes is plenty of sun. If you have a shady yard, don't try to grow a crape myrtle. You'll be disappointed. It will grow in average garden soil, but if you give it a rich, humusy soil, it will be spectacular. You should mulch around it with well-rotted compost, especially while it is still a young bush. It is fairly drought resistant and needs to be watered only in extremely dry periods.

Crape myrtle blooms on the tips of the branches in little ruffles of color, so the more tips you have, the more blooms. Therefore there is a need for pruning, and this pruning should be done right after flowering. If it is a new, young plant, prune it rather severely for the first few years. This will make a bushy growth and give the plant time to get a good root system established. Later, if you wish, you can prune more lightly so that it will develop into a tree. When it becomes large, your crape myrtle may be difficult, or even impossible, to prune, and although you'll have the tree and some blooms, the latter won't be so abundant as on the tree pruned in late summer each year.

Crape myrtles are attacked by a couple of ailments. The one most often seen is mildew. You can control it by spraying either when the buds first start to swell or when they really start to grow. Don't wait too long, or the mildew will stunt their growth and, naturally, affect the bloom. Use either Mildex or Karathane at the ratio of 1 ounce to 25 gallons of water. You have to do this early in the summer before the temperature reaches 85°. During the plant's dormancy you can use a lime-sulphur mixture in a 1–80 dilution to stop the problem before it starts.

The crape myrtle's other affliction is smut. This is a fungus that grows in the honeydew secreted by white flies. If you spray after bloom with malathion at a rate of 3 tablespoons to 3 gallons of water you ought to get rid of it. Another method is to cut off and burn the affected parts.

It is easy to propagate your own crape myrtle and now is the time to do it. Take hardwood cuttings from the tip of a branch 5 to 8 inches long, remove most of the leaves, and put them in a rooting bed or clay pot. The rooting mixture can be all sand, part sand and part peat moss, or part sand, peat, and garden loam. It should be kept damp and in a shady location. When the cuttings develop roots in a few weeks, move them to another area where they will get food. There is none in the peat and sand mixture.

Crape myrtles are also good trees for pleaching, but that's another kettle of fish, and not one to be tackled by the beginning gardener.

Pleaching is the term used for planting two parallel rows of trees to form an avenue narrow enough for the branches to grow across it and into each other forming a "roof" or arbor. The limbs are trimmed higher inside the avenue than on the outside to make an arch overhead, producing the ultimate in gardening reserved for those who are wealthy enough to own plenty of space and a gardener to maintain it. It is not a project for a beginning gardener, but when your ship does come in and you design a pleached arbor, consider using the crape myrtle.

Second Week
IRISES

When I first started talking about and studying about the iris several years ago, I was like the youngster assigned an essay on penguins: I found out more than I really wanted to know.

I already knew them to be beautiful, easy-to-grow flowers that sooner or later find their way into everyone's garden. I knew, too, that you can't throw them away, because wherever they land they'll anchor themselves and go right on growing.

125

Now is the time to separate old clumps or plant new irises. This really should have been done immediately after flowering so that they would have as long as possible to settle in their new home before next year's bloom, but you can still do it. The period of time usually considered best for moving irises is between the first of July and Labor Day, the earlier the better. If you wait and move them in the spring, you'll probably sacrifice that year's bloom.

The iris has been with us a long time and is grown around the world in the northern temperate zone. It was the incarnation of the goddess Iris to the ancient Greeks, it was the royal symbol of France, where it was called fleur-de-lis, and it is still a favorite decorating design. It is one of our most beautiful flowers and a mainstay of the perennial garden.

There are many types of irises, but we don't want to get into that. They can be divided into four general groups. Some grow from rhizomes and include (1) the bearded, both tall and dwarf varieties; (2) beardless, such as the Japanese and Siberian; and (3) the crested; others (4) grow from a bulb, such as the Dutch iris. The most commonly grown iris is the tall bearded. The upright petals are called the standards, and those that grow downward with the little fuzzy streak along the center (the beard) are the falls.

The iris year begins in summer. New rhizomes can be ordered from catalogs, but a quicker way to get irises is to put out the word that you would like some and everybody and his brother will be beating a path to your door with plants.

Your irises will need full sun. Some varieties will bloom in slight shade, but not many. The planting site should be well drained, even if you have to build it up with extra soil.

Into a bed of good garden soil mix some humus, about ½ pound of 5-10-5 commercial fertilizer per square yard, or if you are planting only a group, use about ½ cup for 6 or 7 rhizomes, peat moss, rotted manure, bone meal, wood ashes, and any other organic matter you have. This is not to say they won't live without all this, but they just do better with it.

If you are separating a clump, be sure each piece has a fan of leaves which should be cut off to about 6 or 8 inches. They can be planted in a straight line, but a more pleasing arrangement is to put three to a group, 15 inches apart, with the leaves pointing outward. This may seem far apart, but you don't want to have to move them again next year, and at this distance you can probably get by two or three years before dividing.

Scoop out a shallow place, make a little bump, place the rhizome on it, spread the roots out evenly, then cover with not more than an inch of soil. They'll probably do just as well if you cover only the roots and leave the rhizome partly exposed. Now soak the ground thoroughly and mulch with straw, ground leaves, or whatever you have. Irises don't demand a lot of water except during their blooming period, and then you should give them plenty.

That's about all there is to it. They should bloom next spring.

After they bloom, cut off the stalks several inches above the ground and remove the dried leaves as they occur. Keeping the area around the iris clean is the best insurance against the several insects, especially the iris borer, that can attack the plant.

If you want more adventure, iris plants can be grown from seed, but they won't bloom for two or three years.

The first year after transplanting into good soil your iris may get by without feeding, but each year afterward they should get two feedings during their growth periods. Using 5-10-10 fertilizer, give each large clump about ½ cup in early spring and then about ¼ cup about four weeks after blooming. Sprinkle this on the ground above and around the root spread; don't put it directly on the plant or rhizome. Water well as you should do after any fertilizing.

Irises have many uses in the garden. Many folk plant them in rows by themselves where they are really spectacular, but I think a curved row might be better than a straight one. Because of their pretty foliage they are attractive even when not in bloom. They are invaluable in the perennial border. When used this way, they are usually better planted in clumps, rather than in a solid row. They are excellent beside a pool, along a drive, in front of a wall, in a foundation planting, or as an accent plant beside a tree or large rock, and, of course, in large beds by themselves.

Irises are available in almost every color, so choose the ones you like best or those that complement your home when you use the flowers inside. As a rule, the lighter shades look better in a large planting; save the dark ones for accent plants.

Of the other groups, the Dutch iris should always be planted in large groups if a show is to be made, using at least a dozen bulbs in a grouping. The flat-blossomed Japanese iris is becoming more popular but requires more water than the tall bearded ones.

Once you start giving real care to your irises and see what marvelous plants they are, you may want to join the American Iris Society, which issues a quarterly bulletin and an annual list of iris registrations.

Third Week
GERANIUMS

Late summer has come; the school systems and America's young have returned to the conflict, drawn arms and prepared to do battle. It is safe to estimate that of all the Piedmont's classrooms not more than a dozen will be without a geranium.

There must be a code set down by school authorities that a pot of red geraniums is standard equipment to develop the proper learning environment.

Everybody knows geraniums, those beauties in shades of red, pink, fuschia, and white. They have as many uses as any other flower, and a great many more than most. Once grown only in pots, geraniums have moved into almost every garden location. They can be grown directly in the ground in beds and borders where they offer rich foliage and bright blooms all summer long. They can be used as a summer border. They are at home in the rock or wall garden, and some varieties, because of a pleasant fragrance, are needed in the herb garden. The ivy geranium is happiest in a hanging basket or trailing from a window box. Raised planters, tubs, and sunny spots among shrubs all make happy homes for these bright plants.

But nobody is perfect, and the nonhardy geranium is the first victim of Jack Frost. If your plants are in pots, preserving them is simply a matter of moving them inside in late fall before a frost. Don't put them in a place that is too warm. The ideal location is a sunny window where the temperature is between 50° and 60°.

After they are moved inside, you may find they don't bloom as much as they did outside or may not bloom at all. Don't get alarmed about this. The poor things are tired from all that summer blooming and need a rest, although they don't go into a completely dormant period by dropping all their leaves as some plants do. Keep them in sunlight and water only lightly so you won't encourage too much growth during this rest period. You might even prune them back a bit. After a while they will start growing and bloom again.

If you want plants to bloom inside during winter, start cuttings in May or a little later. It takes about six months from cutting to bloom, which means if you take cuttings even this late, you should have blooms by next February.

If your beauties are outdoors, you will want to save some for blooming inside later in winter and especially for replanting next spring. There are three ways you can preserve the plants.

The first is the easiest. As late as you can before frost hits, pull the plants, tie a string around the stems, and hang them upside down in a dark pantry or storage room where the temperature doesn't drop below freezing.

According to my neighbor Ruth Stephens, this really works because she has done it. They get all dead looking, but they'll snap back when the proper time comes. She says that even before it is time to set them in the ground again, they will begin developing tiny green buds.

The second method is to pot the whole plant and bring it inside. Prepare a pot large enough for the plant with a potting medium of rather rich garden soil and rotted manure. Plants in pots need somewhat richer soil than those in the ground. Lift the plant, put into pots, and prune the limbs back severely, leaving about three large canes 4 or 5 inches high. Keep the soil damp but not soggy. Give them a sunny window, and they should begin to grow again soon. By the time they are large enough to bloom, they will have had the "rest" they need, but if you want stronger plants to go into the spring, pick off the earliest flower buds so that the plant's efforts will go into making a strong plant rather than blooms.

A third method of keeping your favorite geraniums, and getting more plants for next spring than either of the two above, is by taking soft stem cuttings.

Collect several large pots or cans and fill with coarse sand. Take 4-inch cuttings from the geranium plant, using a sharp knife or razor blade so the stem won't be squashed, and cut about ¼ inch below a node, the little swelling on the stem.

Remove all leaves except the top two or three and put about ⅓ of the cutting down into the sand. Several cuttings can be put in one pot. Water well and keep damp until roots form, which will be in two to six weeks. The rooting pots can be kept outside in a light location with good air circulation, but not in direct sun.

When the roots are about ½-inch long, repot each cutting into a 3-inch pot containing garden soil and sand. This first potting mixture should not be too rich. These can still be kept outside until it gets near frost time, then they should be brought inside.

130

You can root the cuttings in water, but the roots get all tangled and don't transplant as well. You can also use vermiculite instead of sand.

Buying a large number of geranium plants for outdoors is somewhat like buying gold bars, so try propagating some over the winter. You'll find it fun.

Fourth Week
DRYING FLOWERS

Before my first effort at drying flowers, I decided I should talk to somebody who knew more than I did. The somebody was Mrs. Sam Stephens, Ruth, who had told me about her geranium-hanging experiences. She was very enthusiastic about preserving summer flowers.

The year before, she used a product, silica gel, which is a blue, granular material somewhat coarser than salt that draws moisture from a flower, leaving its color and shape. The material is sold by the pound and is rather expensive initially, but it lasts for years. When it becomes damp, you put it into the oven according to the directions until it's dry and the blue color restored. Then it's ready to use again. It may be hard to find, but your garden store will order it for you. Some garden catalogs offer it under various trade names. One is Flower Dri.

You will need an airtight container, such as a large potato chip can or a cake tin left from last Christmas' fruit cake.

Ruth says the flowers may be cut at any time of day after the dew has dried in the mornings. Cut perfect flowers, and they should be absolutely dry. She brushes each with a soft brush to remove any dust, insects, or other stuff.

Cut the stem to ½ inch, put some of the gel in the bottom of the tin, put in the flowers face up or down, depending on the nature of their growth, cover completely with the gel, then put the top on the can. Set them aside and in about three weeks they will be dry.

When the flowers are dry, insert a piece of wire through the center of the bloom from the top, making a little hook about ¼ inch from the end so it will catch when you pull the wire through. Wrap your "stem" with green florist tape and your flower is ready for arranging. Use styrofoam or dry foam in your container to hold the flowers.

Ruth has dried marigolds, zinnias, and chives by this method and says colors stay almost exactly natural. She has seen roses and camellias dried beautifully but has not done any. In preserving these two, you will have to be very careful to work the material down between the petals.

"How long will these last?" I asked, and she replied that the ones she did late last summer are still as pretty as when they were finished.

Mrs. Roy Barrett of Pendleton, S.C., has also used this drying method with great success. She and Ruth have lent each other the gel mixture so that more flowers could be prepared.

The method I am using is similar and cheaper. Follow the same procedure for gathering, cutting the stem, etc., then mix 1 part dry sand and 2 parts borax, the kind you get at the grocery store. These should really be well mixed. You can use any kind of shallow box, such as a dress or shoe box; it doesn't have to have a cover. Put some of the sand-borax mixture in, put the flowers on it, and cover with at least 1½ inches of the mixture. Be sure the stuff is worked down between the petals. Put the box in a well-ventilated place. They will dry faster in hot, dry weather than in damp, but they should be dry in from three days to a week, depending on the humidity. If they still seem damp, put them back for a few more days.

If you aren't going to arrange them just yet, put them in a flat box with a ball of paper under each stem near the bloom so that the head is suspended in air. Sprinkle around a bit of the drying mixture to discourage dampness.

Ruth said she tried drying with the borax and sand mixture one year, but the flowers mildewed. She thinks it was because they were damp when she put them in the mixture.

Another method of drying she has used is to hang bunches of flowers upside down in a dark place. She has dried dusty millers like this. Blue salvias, strawflowers, celosias, goldenrods, and canna leaves can all be preserved in this way. Remove the leaves before you hang the flowers because the leaves will get dry and brittle.

You can preserve woody plants such as magnolia, forsythia, and dogwood by first crushing the stem so it will take up more liquid and then standing it in a glass or jar with a 2-inch-deep solution of 1 part glycerine and 2 parts water. It will take about two weeks for these to be properly cured. You can use this mixture over and over again by adding more water.

By preserving your own foliage and flowers, you can enjoy your gardening labors all year and not depend on those man-made plastic and silk flowers to bring color to your home.

Notes for August

September

First Week
PEONIES

One fall the man at the garden store tried earnestly to sell me some peony roots. I suspect that he was not so interested in the beauty of my garden as he was in not having the tubers left at the end of the planting season. To aid his possible sale, he extolled the loveliness of the plants grown by our neighbor a frog's jump away, the late Mrs. Winfield K. Sharp of Sandy Springs, S.C. I called her about her peony culture.

Peonies belong in every garden. They possess almost every qualification a good perennial should have. They are permanent, often outlasting nearby shrubs and other perennials. They are stationary; they rarely need dividing; and they never go spreading all over the place, taking up the whole garden, as some plants do. They produce beautiful blooms in colors from solid white through the pinks and roses to deep red. There are newer varieties in shades of cream, pale yellow, and yellow and white mixed. Peonies are good cut flowers and because their foliage is attractive throughout the summer they look good even when not in bloom.

If you looked hard for a fault in the peony, the only one you can almost count on is that its early summer blooming period is so short; but there are varieties that bloom at different times, so the period of bloom can be extended.

Mrs. Sharp had a special plant. It was a pink one she brought from the home of her mother, the late Mrs. Francis Joseph Hopkins. Mrs. Sharp said she moved it every year for about ten years until she found the proper soil and exposure, and it has been happily blooming in the same location for several years now. This particular plant dates from about 1925, which makes it over 65 years old, Mrs. Sharp said. It seems that in 1937 her parents moved to Seneca on "old Methodist Hill" next door to Mrs. John Barron. Now both Mrs. Hopkins and Mrs. Barron set great store by their flower gardens, and Mrs.

Barron gave Mrs. Hopkins this peony which she had had for many years, and Mrs. Hopkins, in turn, gave a division to her daughter.

Mrs. Sharp called it her "surprise flower" because the color varied each year. She had some advice about growing peonies after her experience with this one and others. First, peonies require at least a half day of sun and should not be planted too close to trees that will take all the soil nutrients. The peony usually grows 2½ feet high and as wide, and should be placed about 3 feet from its neighbor, both for adequate sun and for breathing space.

Mrs. Sharp said she dug a large hole (one book says 18 inches across and as deep), filling it with animal compost and rich garden soil. The peony has a soil requirement of pH 6.0 to 8.0, with 7.0 being a neutral soil. They put down deep roots, which accounts for the large hole of prepared soil. Because of the permanence you aren't going to be moving the thing every year, so take the time to set it out properly, even if you can. get out only one or two plants a year.

Peonies should be planted in the fall, preferably September. Even then they may require a second season's growth to produce blooms. The general rule for moving perennials is to plant in the fall those that bloom in the spring, and to plant in the spring those that bloom in summer and fall, which is only common sense. Still, plan to put out your peonies in September or early October for early summer bloom.

Because they are such heavy feeders, peonies require fertilizing both regularly and heavily. Mrs. Sharp said she fertilized as soon as they put out growth in the spring, using whatever fertilizer happened to be available on the family farm. One year she used ammonium nitrate because that was what was available, and while she was at it, she scattered some among her roses and found that it really made things grow. She added rotted manure each spring and mulched the peonies with humusy soil from the woods or with pine needles.

Peonies demand a dormant period, which is why they don't grow too well in the deep, deep South where the winters are very mild.

One of the major reasons peonies refuse to bloom is that they are planted too deep. Although most authorities say to have the crown not more than 2 inches below the ground, Mrs. Sharp maintained that here in our Southland they should be barely covered, certainly not more than an inch. If possible, the hole for your peony should be prepared a couple of weeks before planting to allow the soil to settle. If planted in a newly prepared place, sometimes the settling results in the roots being covered more deeply than they should be.

As any other plants, they respond to an adequate water supply, but the mulch helps conserve what you do put on. They also need good drainage and won't survive in a constantly damp location.

Mrs. Sharp also advised disbudding. When the buds are about the size of a pea, pinch off all except the top one to get a much larger bloom. Some gardeners prefer more blooms and don't disbud, but if you want a spectacular blossom you might try it. This applies only to the Chinese doubles; nothing is gained by disbudding singles or Japanese varieties.

Peonies make gorgeous cut flowers. They should be cut in early morning or late afternoon and immediately placed in a container of warm water. Because they have a woody stem, you should slit them several times on the end or crush them with a hammer so they will take up more water. Leave the flowers for several hours in a cool place, if you can find a *cool* place in May and June, before you arrange them.

Peonies are spectacular in the garden, but don't impose on their good nature by neglecting them. As with any other flower, they respond to good soil, cultivation, fertilization, mulching, and watering by giving you the years of beauty you expect.

The latest chapter in the Barron-Hopkins-Sharp peony story is that now Mrs. Sharp's daughter Mrs. Tom Gaylord and her children live in the old family home and the peony plant still blooms each summer.

Second Week
PROPAGATION BEDS

If you are out of something to nag your husband about and have been casting around in your mind for a suitable topic, try demanding a propagation bed. There are several things to recommend it: it isn't expensive; it does require some labor, as do most garden endeavors, but this will be good for his spare tire, if not for his disposition; it is economical, saving him money when you don't have to buy baby plants; and it is a good conversation piece, ranking up there with politics and religion.

I once attended an ornamental-plants seminar headed by Frank Fleming, who was our area's Extension Agent for ornamentals, another of the gifts of the Department of Agriculture, and he told us how to do the whole thing.

Mr. Fleming declared that with a little effort we could put the nursery people out of business by propagating our own plants. Now that seems a rather un-Christian thing to do, but since growing plants from little sticks is not everybody's cup of tea, the nurserymen are still safe. But, still, you might want to try your hand at it. The expense is very small, and if you succeed, as you should if you follow his excellent instructions, you will be able to plant your grounds much more generously than if you had to purchase the plants.

All of these suggestions are more or less what he said.

First, determine the location and size of the bed. It should be in filtered shade, never full sun. The bed should be no more than 4 feet wide so you can work it from both sides without having to step into the bed. You may make it as long as you like, but a good working size suggested by Mr. Fleming is 4 x 8 feet, which will hold 200 or more cuttings. If your lot is small, you may want to do a 4-foot-square bed at the beginning.

Second, remove all roots, rocks, etc., from the area so that the soil is fairly smooth.

Third, edge your bed with some material such as logs or boards. This will protect the seedlings and the covering can be nailed to it.

Fourth, dig the bed thoroughly. You can do this with a pick, shovel, tiller, or a teenage son, whichever is the most convenient, but get it all chopped and mixed. You may want to remove some of the soil under the topsoil for the next reason.

Fifth, make the soil looser for the little roots by adding 25 gallons of coarse sand and 3 cubic feet of peat to each 4- x 8-foot section. Don't use fine sand; the kind that comes from creek beds is good. If you don't have a neighborhood creek bed, buy river sand or coarse sand from a builder's supply house. You may use vermiculite instead. Mix the peat and sand with the soil by thoroughly digging and turning to a depth of 8 inches so that the whole bed of soil is loose and fine.

Sixth, level the bed with the back of your rake and soak it thoroughly. You'll find that the peat will absorb and hold a large amount of water.

Now the fun begins.

Seventh, take cuttings about 5 inches long from azaleas, crape myrtles, and other ornamentals. Remove all but the top five or six leaves. Mr. Fleming says the stem won't root without the leaves. Using a sharp knife, cut across the bottom on a slant and dip the cut end into a rooting hormone. There are several rooting hormones on the market under different brand names; they are inexpensive and assure success. After all that work, you want to give your little cuttings every advantage in getting off to a good start. With a pencil or handy stick, make a little hole in the damp propagation bed, insert the cutting about 1½ inches deep or about ⅓ the cutting's length, push the soil firmly around it, and go on to the next one. Set the cuttings about 2 inches apart so that they don't touch, and be sure you don't bury any of the foliage.

Eighth, make a frame of chicken wire (or some such material) tall enough to clear the cuttings when they grow.

Ninth, cover the whole thing with clear plastic, closing the ends and weighting the plastic on all sides to keep out air. This is easiest done by putting a board or rocks around the edge, then piling soil on top of them to make it airtight.

Tenth, wait.

The cuttings should begin rooting in about two or three weeks. The water will evaporate, collect on the plastic and fall back onto the plants. You might check it every couple of weeks to see if it needs additional water, but it probably won't. Keep the plastic cover on all winter until after frost is gone next spring, then remove it a little while each day so the plants can harden.

Eleventh, the day has come. You may plant the rooted cuttings directly into your beds then, or move them to a distance of a foot apart and let them grow, uncovered, in the propagation bed another year. If you decide to do this, you will need to give them a light feeding of liquid fertilizer.

Mr. Fleming said you can follow the same steps using a flowerpot if you want only a few cuttings. Set the pot in a plastic bag, bend a clothes hanger to make a little frame, and bring the plastic bag up, tying it at the top.

Take cuttings from the current year's growth after it has hardened, which means July to September. If you wait much past September, they won't have time to root and get established before cold weather arrives.

Third Week
FLOWERING TREES

Maybe you ought to plant a small tree this fall or winter. It's still a bit early, but if your household is like mine, by the time you decide to do it, buy or order the tree, determine where to put it, and dig the hole, it will be time.

A tree is a marvelous thing. This is from a woods lover who spent a large part of her first twelve years in a backyard pecan tree. My methods of leaving my tree perch varied from swinging on a rope, to dropping from a branch, to falling.

In addition to children, indoor plumbing, electric lights, and a Bible, every house needs trees. Normally the large trees are placed to the sides and rear of the house, not in the front, which blocks the public's view. In addition to these large shade trees, there are many small flowering trees that fit into small yards. Sometimes a tall, slender tree can be used as successfully as a shorter one if the spread is about the same.

Most often the small flowering trees are used for specimens at a distance from the corner of the house, on the sides, or scattered about on the lawn. As specimens, the true shape and beauty of these small trees can be seen as they are set far enough apart to grow freely without bumping into other trees.

There are many reasons for selecting certain varieties. Some, like the flowering peach, have flowers; other, such as the fan-shaped leafed ginkgo, are preferred for their distinctive leaves; still others, such as the holly and downy hawthorn, have berries or fruit that is relished by birds and squirrels. Some trees have more than one of these desirable features, such as the dogwood with its beautiful spring blooms, and red fruit and leaves in the fall. Most of these trees are attractive in leaf even after the bloom has gone, and the bare limbs of winter are in themselves not unattractive.

Don't believe everything you read in nursery catalogs. I have a smoke tree, really more of a large shrub than a tree, that was supposed to "bloom in June." They neglected to say which June. It has come through about twenty Junes, and although the dark foliage is attractive, I have yet to see any smoke or bloom. Some trees require several years of growth before they start to bloom, and maybe this is true of my smoke tree. I hope I live

143

long enough to see this one bloom. I tell you this so that if you do plant a flowering tree, don't expect to be the envy of the whole neighborhood the first spring because of its magnificent blooms. It may take a few years.

Most flowering trees are deciduous, meaning they lose their leaves in winter and go into a dormant stage. Most of them are usually sold bare rooted for planting during this dormancy period, although the larger ones may be balled and wrapped in burlap.

You probably knew this next statement was coming, but before you put out any kind of tree, whether cottonwood, crabapple, or chinaberry, prepare your soil. Dig a hole about 2 feet wider than the balled plant and take out some of the clay if you have it in your yard. Some fellow made a test, and bare-rooted trees planted with damp peat around the roots in the hole made faster and healthier growth than those without it. You can also add humus from your compost pile. You might add some well-rotted manure, but don't mix commercial fertilizer with the planting soil because it might come in direct contact with the tiny roots and burn them.

When you've planted your new little friend, leave a saucer-shaped depression around it to hold water. This has two purposes: first, obviously, it gets water to the plant, and second, it firms the soil around the roots.

It may half kill you to do this, but lop off about a fourth or even a third of the tree to compensate for the root loss during transplanting.

Two other points might be useful. A tree loses water by transpiration through the leaves and evaporation through the bark. You can wrap the trunk in burlap for the first season to prevent dryness and protect it from crawling, chewing things and from bicycles—and also, at least partly, from lawn mowers. If a tree is fairly large, you may have to put up guy wires, but if you don't keep them taut so that they will prevent the tree from swaying and disturbing its roots, you may as well not bother.

144

After all this is done, mulch the tree with pine needles, ground leaves, sawdust, or whatever you have handy. This mulch will keep down the weeds and keep in the water.

There are many small flowering trees or trees with distinctive foliage from which you can choose. Crape myrtle (*Lagerstroemia indica*) blooms for several weeks, sometimes growing to 30 feet with a spread of 10 to 15 feet. It needs sun and rain and comes in shades from white to watermelon red.

Dogwood (*Cornus florida*) is another favorite in shades of pink, white, and more rarely, red. Other plants you might consider are loquat (*Eriobotrya japonica*), American holly (*Ilex opaca*), golden-rain tree (*Koelreuteria paniculata*), flowering crabapple, sourwood (*Oxydendrum arboreum*), flowering cherries, Bradford pear (*Pyrus calleryana* Bradford), European mountain ash, flowering peach, saucer magnolia (*Magnolia soulangeana*), Washington hawthorn (*Crataegus cordata*), mimosa (*Albizia julibrissin*), tree lilac (*Syringa amurensis japonica*), pussy willow, sassafras, Japanese maple, serviceberry, eastern redbud, persimmon, Russian olive, and franklinia.

Fourth Week
SHREDDERS

If anyone asked me point blank whether I would keep my Ed or my shredder, I suppose in a final decision I would keep Ed, but I would think about it awhile first.

Now you don't have to have a shredder. Neither do you have to have an electric or gas range, but they contribute to your cooking ease. You could use a camp fire and a forked stick. The shredder, like the modern stove, is mighty nice to have. I have used one for several years and after each use I go about looking for people who will listen to my praise of it. The only problem is finding the time to use it.

Shredders are not for everybody, but if you have a yard of any size and especially if your lot has trees, you'll find that the shredder-grinder is a good investment, ranking not too far down the line from your lawn mower.

These grinding machines come in many sizes and prices. They aren't usually carried as regular stock in stores but can be ordered from farm-supply houses, garden stores, mail-order catalogs, and directly from manufacturers who advertise in garden magazines. Mine came from the latter. I would suggest you look at several before you buy because even the least expensive is a sizable investment, and you want to be sure you're getting the size machine you need.

The smallest gasoline-driven machine will serve the needs of the average gardener. You can buy machines that attach to your garden tractor, if you have one, and save the cost of an engine. More expensive electric models are available. In addition to the shredder, most companies offer little carts for catching the ground material, and some have vacuums for getting the leaves into the hopper without all that bending. All these little goodies add a considerable amount to the shredder's cost.

One of the first requirements for owning a shredder is a teenage son to help put the thing together when it arrives in a million pieces, stamped encouragingly, "easily assembled." Had it not been for our Tom, mine would still be sitting in its packing case after all these years. Actually there aren't that many parts to be put together, mostly the handle, hopper, protective coverings, etc., but these seem overwhelming to a person who has trouble changing a light bulb.

You'll also need someplace to store it. Most shredders claim to be rustproof, but it's only common sense that they will last longer and perform better if they are given proper care. Because most gasoline models use the same type engine as a lawn mower, your shredder will require about the same maintenance.

Before you invest in this piece of equipment you should

know your purpose. From my experience the two major uses of a shredder-grinder are to grind materials for mulching and for the compost heap. The shredder will quickly turn oak and other leaves into little ¼-to-½-inch pieces that make excellent mulch for shrubs. However, most of your ground-up material will probably go into your compost heap where it will break down much faster than if left whole. Shredding also reduces the bulk of your material to about an eighth of its original size. A mountain of leaves will end up only a few baskets of ground material.

It may sound elementary, but if you are planning to buy a shredder, you should have something to shred. If you have a garden, your shredder will make quick work of your corn stalks, vines, weeds, etc., but most gardeners use it primarily for grinding leaves. If you have only a few trees, it may be necessary to get leaves from your neighbors who will probably be more than glad for you to haul them away. Your shredder will also tackle shrubbery prunings, bean shells from freezer activities, corn husks, and most any organic matter. If your soil is as hard as a rock, you can break it out in chunks, run them through the grinder, then mix the ground soil with peat, humus, or such to loosen it before replacing it in the hole.

Operating the shredder is good therapy. If you're angry with someone, you can feed your shredder with vengeance, pretending you are poking the offending party into the machine head first. This is much preferred to taking a poke at the person himself. Operating the machine can fascinate you, and you'll find yourself resenting telephones, visitors, or anything else that interrupts the morning you had planned to run your grinder.

Running the machine is relatively safe. About the only precaution is to keep your hand and arm out of the hopper and to watch out for any rocks the machine may eject.

Although shredders have been used by commercial nurserymen for more than thirty years, it is only within the last few years that a size to fit the needs of home gardeners has become

147

available. Serious gardeners, especially those who follow the organic way, consider a shredder a necessity instead of the luxurious toy the half-hearted gardener might find it.

You wives may want to ask for a shredder-grinder for Christmas. It's not a two-carat diamond, but it makes a bigger package.

Notes for September

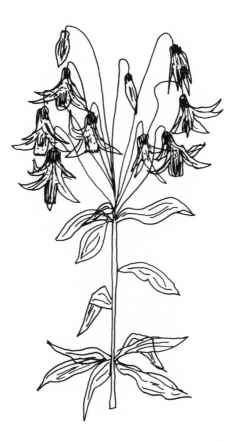

October

First Week
HERBS

"Feel how sore it is," Lee whined, coming home with an ache in the throat parts. After "feeling how sore it was" and listening to her description of the terribleness of the whole thing, I decided I had best do something about the child's sore throat. I got out my home remedy book and looked up a concoction of equal parts onions and molasses.

I don't want to steal comedian Sam Levenson's story about his mother's having a miracle drug—castor oil. Whenever she approached a sick child with the bottle and a spoon, the youngster started yelling, "I'm well! I'm well!"

My remedy worked. After one dose there wasn't another word about sore throats. I may have permanently eliminated this as a health problem in our household.

Some remedies and herbs do have a lot of medicinal value, although maybe not in this particular incident. Many "modern" drugs are herbs in a plastic bottle with a prescription number and a high price tag.

Planting an herb garden has been one of my "going to's" for many years. If you are interested in doing so, you would benefit from visiting one first. There is one at Ashtabula Plantation near Pendleton, S.C., and the Clemson Garden for the Blind has a variety of herbs near the cabin. The finest I've seen is the one at Williamsburg, Virginia. Having visited these public gardens, I decided to try a personal one and called Ada (Mrs. Sam) Moorhead who, someone said, "has the best herb garden in town." She very hospitably invited me over but was very apologetic about just having cut back most of the plants.

Her garden is in two parts. The fragrant garden with mints, tea olive, rosemary, and others is inside a fenced area at the front entrance. The other half, containing mostly medicinal and culinary herbs all mixed together, is at the back door on a slope.

153

While we looked at the many plants, she gave some general suggestions for a successful herb garden.

First of all, she insists, it should be located in full sun. There are a few herbs such as bloodroot, snakeroot, and digitalis that will live in shade, and others, including balm, tarragon, the mints, comfrey, cotsmary, ginger, and lemon verbena that will endure partial shade, but to really thrive, the herb garden should have as much sun as possible.

Second, the soil should be loose, friable, slightly humusy, and rich. Ada said that herbs are usually considered tolerant of average soils, but her experience has been that the better the soil, the better the herbs.

Third, they need water—and adequate drainage. For this reason she has moved many of her plants from the planned garden in the front to the sloping location at the rear of the house. She has about thirty different herbs.

Many of the herbs such as thyme, basil, oregano, chive, mint, and others, she uses in cooking. Others she keeps primarily for fragrance. Some have medical uses, but she doesn't use them for that, instead keeping them because of the attractiveness of the plant or for the fragrance. In this group go wormwood, camphor, tansy, cardoon, and silver king artemisia.

Like many other cooks, Ada prefers the fresh or home-dried herbs to those bought in stores. She uses many in soups, sauces, casseroles, and stews. She breaks the leaves from the plant, rinses them, and drops them in the pot. She freezes dill to use in sauce for fish simply by dropping it in a plastic bag and putting it in the freezer. She dries certain plants such as thyme and cardoon by tying them in bunches and hanging them upside down indoors. If you have large amounts of herbs to dry, one expert suggests putting them in a paper bag and tying the open end around the stems. Hang them upside down indoors. This way the herbs aren't touching anything that would absorb the oils that give the herbs both their fragrance and flavor.

154

Many of her plants are annuals that she starts from seed in the spring. If she moves any of the perennials, she does this in the spring also. In summer the herbs are watered and weeded as any other plant, and in the fall they are harvested. Many of the perennials get woody stems and she cuts them back in the fall.

Her own garden began with seeds and with plants purchased from Pine Hill Herb Farm in Roswell, Georgia. Many nurseries now offer a variety of herb plants.

Among the many herbs Ada grows are several mints: spearmint, curly mint, peppermint, walnut, and orange mint; several thymes, including silver, golden, creeping, and English common; basil, rue, rosemary, dill, balm, wormwood, Egyptian mint, sweet marjoram, and pot marigolds.

If you are considering an herb garden, one of the first things you are likely to face is the question, "Where shall I put it?" Well, first of all, herbs don't have to be in a garden especially designed for them. There are some herbs such as parsley and chives that you can grow in a pot on the window sill. Others such as dill, because of their ungainly size, would hardly be satisfactory for pot culture but are quite at home in the vegetable garden.

You can also grow herbs among your flowers. Most of them have blooms that would add to your garden, but even if they don't, their foliage, especially the gray ones, makes a color contrast to the green plants. This is true of the members of the Artemisia family, such as silver mound and dusty miller, that are often used as accents.

If you want only a few herbs you can easily put a few plants of sage or mint near the back door, at the edge of the porch, near the garden gate, or any other spot. However, should you decide to have a real garden as such, there are many designs you can use.

A word of caution: Don't make your garden too large—8 x 10 feet is large enough unless you are planning to open a shop.

To a gardener accustomed to planting long rows of zinnias and beds of marigolds, the suggestion of two plants of this herb and three of that one may sound unrealistic. Even if you use herbs generously in cooking, you'll find that one bunch of dill will go a long way. The rule of good gardening housekeeping also applies to herbs: Don't plant more than you can care for.

You can be ordinary and plant your herbs in one long row or in short rows side by side. Instead, be adventurous and have a garden design. You can even have a rock garden with herbs. You don't have to have a hillside like Ada, but you do need rocks. Arrange large- and medium-sized rocks on the ground and fill the spaces and crevices among them with good soil, including a touch of lime, then place your low-growing herbs. The rocks will eliminate the need for paths or any separators and also add eye appeal.

In designing your garden your imagination can run wild. Do include paths so you won't have to step on the herbs while weeding and gathering. You can outline your garden with a walk of either hard, bare earth, brick, or stone. You can arrange the plants in little squares, triangles, circles, or whatever design suits your fancy.

To separate the different kinds of herbs use 2 x 6 boards laid flat, bricks, paths, or you can let the plants all run together. Keeping them separated makes a neater garden. There are a few, such as mint, that you might even want to grow in pots set in the ground to prevent their spreading too much.

A favorite design is the herb wheel using an old wagon wheel. The farmer's wife can usually find one stored in a barn somewhere, but the city gardener will have more trouble finding one. Fill the spaces between the spokes with soil and set your plants. You can probably get two different herbs in each section.

If possible put the herb garden near the kitchen door. You'll be more likely to use your herbs if they're nearby, and you'll have the added pleasure of the pungent fragrance whenever you go outside.

After you've made all these plans, you come to the business of selecting the herbs to use. You might begin with the onesyou normally use in cooking or whose fragrance you admire, then go on from there. You should have a special purpose in mind for each herb you plant and not end up with the question, "Now that I've got it what do I do with it?"

This list might help.

Mints—Mint sauce for lamb, use in tea and other drinks, in salads, or sprinkle on fresh fruits. Use the green leaves.

Sage—Mix with pork sausage, in dressing, stuffing, in cheese dishes. Use dried leaves.

Thyme—The most-used herb, use with meat, fish, vegetables, soups, and in stuffings. Use the leaves.

Rosemary—Chicken dishes, soups, stews, venison, rabbit, game birds, in cooking water for peas and potatoes. Use green or dried leaves.

Oregano—A must for roast pork, spaghetti, and other Italian cookery, use in stews and soups. Use fresh or dried leaves.

Basil—Tomato dishes, sprinkle over cooked vegetables, egg and cheese dishes, fish casseroles, in water to cook rice and in spaghetti sauce. Use leaves; harvest before plant blossoms.

Dill—Seeds used in pickles, cakes and dill bread, potato salad, and cole slaw. Harvest "dill weed," the leaves in early summer.

Savory—Meat loaf, hamburgers, for game, fish, and pork, as a garnish. Also beans, soups, stuffings. Leaves from non-blooming plants.

Rue—This is slightly bitter so use it sparingly in tomato or vegetable juices, in salads and stews. Mostly ornamental.

Marjoram—Use in chowders, fish, meat, game, poultry, sprinkle some in gravies and sauces. Use fresh or dried leaves.

Chamomile—Use dried flower heads to make a tea. It's supposed to help whatever ails you.

Bee balm, or bergamot—Tastes a little like lemon. Use dried leaves to sprinkle on roasts, fresh ones in iced tea or fruit cup.

157

Once you start your small herb garden and become accustomed to cooking with herbs, you'll agree that the amount of time spent in planning, planting, and weeding your "yarbs" was a good investment.

Second Week
LILIES

I used to think the only lilies were those held by cartoon corpses and those that annually invaded the church at Easter. That's like saying that the only ice cream flavors are chocolate and vanilla. There are many types and many varieties of lilies. A lot of plants are lumped into the family Liliaceae, including such dissimilar plants as hostas, trilliums, and the day lily, but I am talking about the true lily, *Lilium*.

Most lilies grow between 3 and 6 feet tall and are really spectacular. Some of them are difficult for an amateur, but many are easily grown if you follow the right procedure.

Think carefully before deciding where to put them. First, they can stay in the same place for several years before overcrowding requires digging and separating. A second reason is that the bulbs are expensive. Even the cheapest are four or five dollars a bulb and the newer hybrid varieties can cost many times that. You want to give real attention to such expensive bulbs.

Lilies look best against a background. They can be placed in an open bed, but a brick wall, shrubbery, vine, or other background shows them off better. They also have a delightful fragrance, so don't put them so far away from the house that you don't enjoy it.

Most lilies like sun. There are some such as the gold-banded, orange, Hanson, Henry, and Japanese that do well in partial shade, but as a rule select an area that gets full sun or at least morning sun. They also like good air circulation. This means not to crunch them up in a tight corner or plant too close to a wall. They need both growing and breathing space.

The biggest single enemy of lilies is poor drainage. If you don't believe it, just place a bulb in a shallow bowl of water for a few weeks and watch what happens. The same thing will happen to a bulb planted in a constantly wet location. The drainage problem can be straightened out if you make a little effort. Some people say to dig a deep trench and lay agricultural tile, but I guarantee you that I won't ever do that. You can raise the bed slightly to help the drainage, but there is a still better way.

Dig about 18 inches deep in the bed and partly refill it with part soil, cottonseed meal, bone meal, humus, and sand—all mixed well. Bring this to within 10 inches of the ground level and then put down 2 inches of sand and place your bulb on this and cover. Not all bulbs should be set this deeply, that is, 8 inches, and the depth depends on the growth habits of each particular variety. The layer of sand immediately under the bulbs drains the water, yet the roots will reach through it to the nourishing soil mixture underneath.

Some bulbs form roots along the stem and so should be set about 8 inches or about three times the height of the bulb so there will be enough stem underground to form a strong root system. Lilies that grow this way are the Bateman, Brown, morningstar, orange Hanson, Henry, Japanese, Easter, royal, speciosum tiger, and yellow Martagon.

Others produce roots only from the base of the bulb so should be set no deeper than 4 inches from the top of the bulb to ground level. Some of these are the madonna lilies, turkscap, and Caucasian.

Cover the bulb with the rest of your planting mixture and water thoroughly. They should be given a winter mulch, then in the spring they should get a feeding of 5-10-10 fertilizer or well-rotted manure. You will be wise to put little plant markers in front of the bulbs so you'll know where they are.

159

Bulbs should be planted as soon as they arrive in the fall, if you order them, or as soon as they are available in stores. They can be carried over to spring under certain conditions, but this is tricky and the beginning gardener should get them in the ground in the autumn. Unlike tulips and daffodils, lily bulbs are never completely dormant and should be handled with the same care as growing plants.

In the spring when the shoots appear, mulch them again to keep them moist. This "moist" is not the same as being sopping wet from lack of drainage. Lilies are not particular about soil, and most will live in a neutral one. However, if your lilies develop yellow leaves, it may be because the soil is too alkaline, and well-rotted manure or compost worked around them will help.

Although you will be tempted, don't cut the blossoms more than every other year because this greatly weakens the plant for the following year. Unless you want to plant the seed, remove the blooms as they fade.

Lilies can be grown from seed and many catalogs offer them, but they take about three years to bloom. Plant the seed in the spring in flats or a seedbed and let them stay there two years. The third year set the bulblets into the garden where they will continue to grow.

A friend of mine, Nita Radcliffe, has a lily fancier friend and who gave her a list of lilies that will provide bloom from June until September. I share the list with you.

June blooming: Backhouse hybrid lilies mixture, *L. candidum* (madonna lily), Corsage, Destiny, Enchantment, Golden Chalice hybrids, Harlequin hybrids, Hanson II.

July: Adagio, Black Dragon, Centifolium, Damson, Fire King, Golden Clarion, George Creelman, Green Dragon, Honeydew, Life Moonlight, Pink Perfection, Regal, Anaconda, Bright Star, Prince Charming.

August: *L. auratum macranthum*, Imperial Crimson, etc.

September: *L. longiflorum* (Easter lily).

Because of the wide selections the beginning gardener would probably be safe in selecting *Henryi, Hansoni, Regale, Formosanum, and Speciosum rubrum*. Beautiful new hybrids are introduced each year and the enthusiastic lily grower will watch the catalogs and garden shops for these.

Third Week
FALL-PLANTED ANNUALS

It may be hard to think of next May's sunshine and the lovely fragrance of colorful sweet peas with frost all over October pumpkins, but there is virtue in planning for the future. As with Christmas preparations and making dinner rolls, you can't wait until the last minute with sweet peas.

In our beautiful South, we should plant them in the fall in late October or November, and they will come up early next spring, whereas our northern neighbors plant them in the spring as soon as they can get the snow, sleet, slush, and other such undesirables off the ground.

In addition to sweet peas there are other annuals that should be planted in the fall. There will be warm days of autumn even in November, so on one of these you should do your fall planting.

Among the fall-planted annuals are Shirley poppies, larkspur, cornflower, calliopsis, balsam, bells of Ireland, and, of course, sweet peas. You can still plant hollyhocks if you didn't do it in late summer when you should have.

In addition to being real beauties in the yard, sweet peas make the loveliest cut flowers, filling a room with their marvelous colors and fragrance. And what kind of student is it who can't carry his teacher a vase of sweet peas in spring?

There are two kinds of sweet peas.

There is a perennial vine whose seed is a little hard to find. This vine, *Lathyrus latiofolius*, grows to 8 feet and is quite hardy even to zone four. It isn't at all fragrant and requires a trellis to support its tall growth. Its colors are more limited than the annual appearing only white, pink, and magenta.

The perky sweet pea that most of us know is *Lathyrus odoratus*, the beautiful little fragrant spring plant that everybody loves.

Sweet peas need sun, especially since they bloom early and need its warmth after the winter months, so don't put them in the shade. Don't put them near privet or apples either or they may come down with a case of anthracnose, a disease that is first evident in white spots on the leaves and buds. Soon the buds dry up and fall off. A spraying with Bordeaux will help prevent this and spraying with zineb will help control it.

Sweet peas are extremely heavy feeders and require rich soil for best growth and bloom. You must dig the soil at least 1 foot deep, although 18 inches would be better, and mix in well-rotted manure or compost. Add some bone meal at the rate of 1 pound to 15 feet of row. Sow the seeds about 2 or 3 inches deep and as far apart. Cover and give a light protection with straw, pine needles, or other light mulch. This should be removed in the spring.

If you don't get them planted this month or next and wait until spring, you may want to try the method of making a 6-inch trench in the prepared soil, planting the seed, and covering them with 2 inches of soil. As the plants grow, continue filling the trench until it is ground level.

Next spring, when the plants are about 4 inches high, put inthe stakes if you need them. These don't have to be fancy; broken tree limbs will do because the plants will soon cover them. Don't use wire because it can get so hot that it will injure the plants.

You may have to water.

One reason sweet peas stop blooming is that the blooms are not picked. If they are allowed to form seed pods they no longer make blooms, so for a longer blooming period, keep them cut. If you mulch them, the ground will stay cooler and the blooming season will be further extended.

There are several kinds of sweet peas you might like to try. For years Cuthbertson's Floribunda was considered the best because it is heat resistant and carries five, six, or more flowers per stem and comes in beautiful colors. Recently a new hybrid, the Royal, has challenged Cuthbertson's for first place. Royal blooms longer, has larger stems, and is even more heat resistant—an important consideration in our southern climate. Both of these need staking. A slightly shorter plant that requires no staking is the Knee-Hi sweet pea that grows 2½ feet high with five to seven blooms on each stem. This one is also heat resistant.

There is another sweet pea, the Bijou, which grows only a foot high. This makes it useful for borders, beds, and window boxes where the taller plants would be unsatisfactory. Its colors are bright and clear in shades of crimson, mauve, salmon pink, rose, blue, and blue-violet.

If you want a really tiny plant, there is the Little Sweetheart, a compact little 8-inch bush covered in ruffled flowers of white, cream, pink, rose, and dark-blue shades. Try planting it in front of the taller varieties.

With so many kinds to choose from and such ease in growing, after all the hard digging is done this fall, sweet peas should be in everybody's spring garden. And they can be if you get out and do some work now; the backache will be long forgotten by the time the little beauties bloom next spring.

Fourth Week
COLD FRAMES

It occurred to me that one thing we can do this fall to get ready for spring gardening is to build a cold frame. I have tried to grow seeds in flats inside the house, but have never had much luck. They always get too hot, too dry, too wet, always too something. Success is more likely with a cold frame. Whether you want the frame for vegetables or flowers, you will get great satisfaction from growing your own plants.

You can use either blocks, brick, or wood. If you use wood the best is cypress or redwood, both expensive. Most all garden shops carry salt-treated pine logs called "landscape timbers." These are about three-by-five inches and about eight-feet long. They can be easily stacked two or three high. Lacking these you perhaps can find scrap lumber. None of the wood will last as long as the blocks of course. Don't use wood treated with creosote.

You can make a shallow frame extending only a couple of inches into the ground, but as long as you're into the project, go on and do it properly. If you are using brick or block, you have to excavate the hole and build directly into it. If using wood, build the frame wherever convenient, then dig the hole, put in the frame, and pack dirt around the outside walls.

Select a site on the south side of a building with the low side facing south to catch the sun and the building to the rear to protect the frame from wind.

It can be made most any size and covered with clear plastic, but glass is better. A used window sash is fairly cheap and good for this. Get your sash first and build the frame to fit it. You may hinge the glass or not, but be sure to have it open all the way for easy working inside the frame.

Above-ground height at the front should be a minimum of 6 inches, and the above-ground height at the rear, 12 inches. You can make these higher. The frame should extend 12 inches into the ground. After the structure is in place, fill the hole, or inside of the frame, with 4 or 5 inches of gravel for drainage topped with an inch or so of compost. On top of this goes 3 inches of good garden soil, which in turn is topped with 3 inches of a mixture of good soil, sand, and peat or humus. This will bring the inside level with the outside ground level.

You can use the frame to store nonhardy plants, but in coldest weather you may have to throw on an old rug at night, removing it in the daytime to catch the sun's rays. If the weather is extremely cold, you can mulch the plants with straw or leaves before closing the sash.

Your cold-frame use can begin this fall with the planting of lettuce and radish seed, and with any luck you should have salad makings in a few weeks.

The most common use of a cold frame is for starting seed in early spring. In March, about six weeks before they go outside, plant seeds of annuals, such as petunias, marigolds, salvia, verbena, stock and many others. They may be planted directly into the soil or in flats and set inside the cold frame.

Don't fill the whole space with seed because you'll need some area for transplanting. When the little fellows get a couple of sets of leaves, lift them, make a hole with a pencil in another part of the frame, and replant them an inch or so apart to give them growing room.

You can start cabbage, broccoli, cauliflower, tomato, and other vegetable seed in your cold frame.

Three points of maintenance are necessary.

One, the plants must have water. Water them with a light spray.

Two, they must have light. Keep the glass uncovered to admit sun unless there is a severe cold snap.

Three, they need ventilation. On warm days raise the glass sash an inch or so to let in fresh air. As the days get warmer and the plants get larger and nearer transplanting time in the garden, raise the glass more and more until it stays open all day, allowing the plants to harden off.

After the seedlings move out in May, you can put in cuttings of chrysanthemums. In July you can plant perennial seed such as columbine and foxglove, and put in azalea cuttings. In August you can plant pansies.

Growing plants from seed is much more economical than buying them, and it's fun too—not nearly as much work as it sounds.

So the first Saturday afternoon you see your husband or teenage son sitting around enjoying himself watching the ball game, appeal to his community pride to get up and do something useful—like building a cold frame.

Notes for October

November

First Week
FORCING BULBS

About 15 years ago I tried forcing some bulbs and I couldn't have made a bigger mess if mess-making had been my goal. The bulbs rotted, the water got black and slimy, the closet smelled terrible, the container leaked, and the floor was water streaked. There must be another way, I decided, and left off the bulb-forcing business until another day when I knew more about what I was doing.

The day has arrived, thanks to Arthur and Emma Holman of our town who have been forcing bulbs for indoor bloom for years with great success. They were kind enough to share their methods with me. Emma quickly gives Arthur the credit for the project, although she helps him. Arthur, a local wit known for his easy, quick laughter, insists the whole business couldn't be easier and that even a beginning gardener can have success. I'm glad he didn't see my closet.

Over the years they have forced all kinds of bulbs: tulips, daffodils, calla lilies, paper-white narcissuses; but the ones they use most are hyacinths. They like them because of the colorful blooms and the yummy fragrance that can fill an entire room from only one pot of plants. The hyacinths can be planted immediately after purchasing, but the other bulbs should be kept in the refrigerator at least a week, although several weeks won't hurt them. Don't be a dunce and put them in the freezer; you'll kill the bulb.

The Holmans buy bulbs as soon as they are available in August or September and start planting the hyacinths right away. They refrigerate the others until they get around to planting them. They make plantings at intervals of about a week, doing two or three pots at a time. They use the same kind and color of bulb in one pot.

Using 6-inch clay pots they put gravel for drainage in the bottom then fill it with a mixture of garden soil, well-rotted manure, and 1 tablespoon of bone meal per pot. If you don't have the manure, Arthur suggests using woods' earth, humus, or the purchased composted manure that comes in 25-pound bags.

Next he sets four bulbs in each pot at a depth where the tops are covered by a half inch of soil. The pots are watered well and placed under his house in the dark away from the furnace. The ideal temperature, Arthur said, is about 50°, so a closet or cabinet in the average house is too warm and the bulbs will rot. I know. I know.

The storage place must be cool and it must be dark. This might present a problem to some folks. If your house isn't underpinned or if there is no crawl space, he suggests digging a trench outdoors, setting your pots in it, and covering them with leaves or sawdust until the bulbs sprout. This is obviously hard work, but if you're bigger than everybody else in your house, maybe you can make someone else do the work. It all depends on how eager you are to have the flowers.

Arthur leaves them in the dark, cool storage, watering them once a week until the stems are up and about 2 inches high and especially until the bloom bud is up out of the bulb. If you move them before the bud is out, you'll have little, dinky flowers.

At this stage the leaves and stems are white from being in the dark. Arthur moves the pots indoors, but not in direct sunlight, until the leaves turn green, which takes about a week. When the leaves are green and growing, they move the pots to a sunny window and in a few days the buds open.

After the blooms fade, the pots are set aside and others brought in. Sometime during the next year the bulbs will be moved into the wooded area near their home where they will bloom for several years. They always use new bulbs for forcing.

In addition to all this care, Arthur does have one little secret he shares. He gives each pot 1 teaspoon of superphosphate once a month, which means each pot gets two or three feedings. The superphosphate makes straight, strong stems that can support the heavy bloom.

The time involved in all this varies. The white hyacinth Innocence will bloom from 8 to 10 weeks after it is set out. Others require 12 weeks. By planting at intervals beginning the first of September, the Holmans have blooming plants in the house from the last of November when Jack Frost has pretty well captured everything until February when the early crocuses and daffodils start. They make their last planting about the first week in November and these will bloom in January or February. Bulbs set later will do just as well, but the Holmans like this schedule because it gives fresh flowers in the house during the winter.

Nothing could be simpler, Arthur insists.

Second Week
ORIENTAL POPPIES

Pete and Myrtice Cooper were our good friends and neighbors—pillars of the church, salt of the earth, and all that. I even had him selected as one of my pall bearers, but he said I was mighty optimistic about his health since he was a good many years older than I am. I still grieve over his unexpected passing.

One of my favorite anecdotes about the Coopers concerns his rebuilding the well house located about 300 yards from the home. Mrs. Cooper asked him why, as long as he was building a new one anyway, didn't he put it closer to the residence? He explained gently that he had to put the well house where the well was.

Anyway, the Coopers had some oriental poppies in their front yard that had been there since they moved into our rural community more than 20 years ago. Every year the Coopers, who loved to garden, worked and fertilized them. Every year the poppies responded with many beautiful pink blooms atop the gray-green foliage.

Now is the time to set out oriental poppy roots. If we lived farther north, August would have been the time, but you can still plant here in our beautiful Southland. Don't try to move them at all unless they are dormant or you'll be wasting your time and killing the plants. You can wait until early spring, just when they are putting up new growth, but now is better.

One way to get a start of oriental poppies is to buy roots, and most catalogs offer them. Another way is to get a dormant root, cut it in several 1- or 2-inch pieces, being sure there is a joint on each piece, and root them in sand in your cold frame. They should be ready to transplant in the spring. You can plant seed one year for bloom the following year, but your colors may not run true. Of these ways, the easiest is to buy the root or divide a clump.

This oriental poppy, *Papaver oriental,* requires very little care and will last for years if you will just let it have its way in the beginning of your friendship.

One thing they have to have is full sun. Nothing less will do. They also need a good garden soil with plenty of humus, and it should be somewhat gritty, so mix in some manure, some stuff from your compost heap, and some sand if you can get all that in one spot.

Dig deeply in your well-prepared bed. Try to keep the root out of the ground no longer than necessary. When you have put the root in its new home, cover it with 1 inch of soil. Because the plants grow quite large, set the roots about 2 feet apart and they won't be crowded as they grow. In the fall give them some rotted manure and a good balanced fertilizer such a 4-8-4. And that's about all there is to it.

They do have the disadvantage of dying shortly after they bloom, so the foliage is pretty unsightly by mid-summer. If you plant annuals around them or set them at the middle or back of your border, the drooping leaves will be hidden.

There are several kinds of poppies, both annual and perennial, but the orientals are about the grandest, mainly because of their brilliant blooms that measure 6 inches or more and the long, hairy, gray-green leaves. The colors are not limited to the pinks that the Coopers had but are also available in lavender, red, mahogany, watermelon pink, salmon orange, shell pink, and white.

If you keep the blossoms picked, the blooming season will be lengthened just as with many other flowers. And unless you want poppies growing out of your ears, you had best keep the seed heads picked off, because the plant will self-sow.

Poppies are sometimes used in beds alone, but most often they are used for accent plants in the border. Because of their 3-foot height, they go in the middle section of the bed. They can also be used in a row against a fence or in front of shrubbery if you either plant something in front of them to hide the dying foliage or just accept it.

However you use them, do try poppies. They are dependable year after year with minimum work, and to me that one characteristic makes a good flower.

Third Week
HEDGES

Hedges are not as popular in our area as they are in some parts of the country. They should be used more. One of the reasons people don't use them is that they have to be trimmed, which is a lot of work in our hot southern summers.

But all hedges don't need trimming. There are many plants that do quite nicely without any trimming at all and others that can be clipped or unclipped, depending on the wishes and/or energy of the gardener.

There are a lot of good things about hedges. They keep the neighbors from seeing you; they keep you from seeing the neighbors; and they keep everybody from seeing something you wish to have private, such as the play yard, clothesline, and garbage cans.

Aside from the privacy element, hedges can mark property lines, divide sections of the yard, and define special areas such as rose, herb, and vegetable gardens and the cutting garden for flowers. One excellent use of hedges is to serve as a background for a flower border.

Hedges, like people, can come in all sizes and shapes. It can be a little thing of 1 or 2 feet in height edging the drive or a 10-foot impenetrable mass through which neither bicyclers, burglars, nor borrowers can pass. Privet, if you don't keep it trimmed, can reach 30 feet. There aren't many people, though, who actually need a 30-foot hedge. In some parts of the country people do plant tall hedges to serve as windbreaks, but they aren't usually needed in the South unless you build your house out in the middle of a field.

Decide on the kind of hedge you want before you select the plants. Do you want it high or low, dense or loose, natural growing or neatly clipped? Don't forget to consider the eventual width. A pyracantha or bridal wreath hedge may require a 10-foot width, but a low-clipped box hedge will be only 1½ or 2 feet wide. Consider this especially when planting along a property line. Come well within the line so that when the hedge is grown it won't be sticking over in your neighbor's yard.

The same is true of putting hedges along walkways. If you set the plants right at the edge, as they grow they will fill the walk and every trip to and fro will become an obstacle course for stockings.

There are many plants that can be left unclipped and look quite well. Among these are barberry, viburnum, winged euonymus, Russian olive, lilacs, spirea or bridal wreath, and bush honeysuckle. There are several plants called bush honeysuckle because they grow in bush form, unlike our native vine that grows wild. One of the honeysuckles is *Lonicera fragrantissima* an eight-foot deciduous shrub. Another is *Lonicera nitida*, a compact evergreen that grows four to five feet. This one may be difficult to find.

If you have the time and want the perfectionist look of clipped hedge, choose boxwood, spreading euonymus, or convexa holly (*Ilex crenata "convexa"*) which is sometimes called "boxwood holly" by home gardeners although there is no such creature. The leaves are small and oval like boxwood. Another holly, Japanese holy *Ilex crenata*, makes a good hedge. Also consider juniper, cotoneaster, or privet.

Boxwood, barberry, and Russian olive make a pretty hedge if left untrimmed. So do wintercreeper, colonial spruce, and Hick's yew.

There are several deciduous shrubs that can be planted close to form a hedge. These include flowering quince, Rose of Sharon, mock orange, and lilacs and spirea. Pyracantha makes an almost impassable barrier with its sticky thorns. Its red or orange berries are beautiful in the fall, but because of its huge size if left untrimmed, it's not for small yards.

Most evergreen shrubs should be pruned in early spring right before the growth starts. Rapid growers such as privet will need two or three prunings during the growing season, but for many others this early pruning is sufficient. Flowering shrubs should be pruned immediately after blooming or you'll cut off next year's buds.

Although different plants have different pruning requirements, in general they should be left larger at the base, tapering to a rounded top. Usually, too, a rounded top is more desirable than one that is sheared flat and squared off.

Most hedges require only average soil. The time to fertilize is when you set the plants using a commercial fertilizer or rotted manure. The distance apart that you set the plants depends on how large you want the hedge to grow. A tall hedge should be set 18 to 24 inches apart, but one you plan to trim and keep low can be set as close as 12 inches. If you want a big shrub you have to give it more growing room.

Most shrubs can be planted in either fall or spring, but fall planting gives you a season's extra growth. Consider adding a hedge to your landscaping. You'll be pleased with the finished look it gives your yard.

Fourth Week
GREENHOUSES

A few years ago we moved from our former home just across the highway to our present house, a rambling, hundred-year-old, two-story frame structure which some people call the "old homeplace," but which I prefer to designate the "ancestral manor" of my Ed's family. Preceding the moving were several months of remodeling, mind changing, and harsh words on occasion, so that by the time the actual exodus took place, nobody in the family was speaking to anybody else. We were still in the talking and planning stage, neither hammer nor saw having been drawn, when I asked my Ed if, while we were up to our necks in redoing the kitchen-laundry area, we could build an adjoining greenhouse. My Ed said, "No." He didn't even leave it open for discussion or negotiation. Just, "no."

I think having an attached greenhouse would be the grandest thing. As we all know any kind of greenhouse is a luxury and only a nurseryman or floriculturist could claim he really *needs* one. Still the price is not as prohibitive as it used to be, and one authority says it costs no more than a used car. I still don't have one.

Home greenhouses fall generally into four categories, based on cost and construction.

The most elaborate, usually the largest, and certainly the most expensive, is the freestanding house. It has its own heating system and should be a minimum of 5 x 10 feet. Any smaller type greenhouse cools and heats too quickly to maintain an even temperature. If you're going to all the expense of this type structure, you would do well to make it much larger because only the really serious gardener would build this type.

The second type is the glassed building attached to the house from which it gets its heat. This type, if kept filled with pretty blooming plants, is quite an asset to the attractiveness of the house. It must be built on the south or southeastern side of the house, and there is a doorway from it into the house so that, in effect, it becomes another room.

The third type of greenhouse is a kind of lean-to against the house or other building with the glass slanting to catch the sun, which provides the heat. There is usually a door to the outside rather than one leading into the building it is against.

The fourth kind is a plant window, which is like an all-glass bay window extending beyond the house. It gets its heat from the room. It really isn't much of a greenhouse in the strict sense of the word, but does provide growing space for plants.

There are two other kinds that go somewhere in one of these four groups. The basement greenhouse is an excavation outside the walls of the house with an entrance from the basement. The top is glass covered and from the outside looks like a tall cold frame since most of it is below ground level. Its heat is from the sun and the basement. There is, of course, a door into it from the basement.

Another similar one is a converted old-fashioned root cellar, which many country homes and some city ones have. The top is roofed in glass slanting at a 45° angle toward the south to catch the sun. There is not much heat loss, so a small electric

heater or a couple of high-wattage light bulbs would be sufficient to heat it. The doors should be insulated of course.

Whatever style you build, choose your greenhouse location
with care. It is usually on the south or southeast so that during
December and January it receives the maximum morning sun.

All greenhouses should be built of strong, durable materials.
Concrete, brick, or some kind of masonry is preferred for the
foundation, and during recent years aluminum instead of wood
has become the favorite structural material for the sides and
roof. The initial cost may be more, but it doesn't rust or rot,
saving both painting and replacing. Building a greenhouse is
not an amateur's job; a knowledge of carpentry is necessary.

Although glass would probably be preferred for the attached
greenhouse, sheets of polyethylene film are often used to decrease the cost of a freestanding unit. It isn't as attractive as
glass but has certain advantages. It is much cheaper, has greater
moisture retention and less heat loss. It has only 90 percent the
light transmission of glass, but some plants like this better. It
does deteriorate in bright sun and may have to be replaced often, usually annually. If the greenhouse is the project of a
home-gardener do-it-yourselfer, he will have greater success
with a concrete block foundation, wood frame, and polyethylene film-covered structure than with a brick-and-glass building.
The latter would require the hiring of a brick mason and a
glazier unless the gardener is a right handy fellow. Fiberglass
in panels, rolls, and panes is another substitute for glass. It lasts
about 5 to 15 years and permits about 80 percent of light
to enter.

There are three requirements of a successful greenhouse,
whatever type you have.

The first is heat. Now you can have an unheated structure
and can grow some plants quite well, but for maximum use it
should be heated. The temperature preferences for plants vary
greatly, but a night temperature of 50° to 55°, which means a
daytime temperature of 60° to 75°, is suitable for a wide range

of plants. You can heat with hot water, oil, bottled gas, or electricity, and if you choose the latter, your friendly neighborhood power company may help you design one to fit your needs.

The second is ventilation. Even on cool days the glass should be open a crack. The primary purpose is for reducing and regulating temperature and humidity. Getting in fresh air is secondary because some of that is going to come in through the cracks. Overheating can be a problem even with good ventilation. This is especially true in late fall when the night temperature drops to the 30s and the day temperature may reach the 60s or 70s.

The third is humidity. In addition to actually watering the plants, which is best done with a fog nozzle, the whole interior should be humid. This is most easily achieved by fogging the whole greenhouse. Watering the floors helps also unless yours is a window greenhouse without a floor.

Shading is something else you may need to consider especially if you grow a lot of shade-loving plants. You can buy this in rolls. It is a woven, plastic material that can be used for several seasons.

Your major use of the greenhouse will probably be to grow out-of-season tomatoes or lettuces and to start cuttings and seeds. If your greenhouse is really large you can grow tropical plants but most home greenhouses aren't big enough to accommodate shrubs. Greenhouses here in the Piedmont usually see service in fall, winter, and early spring and are pretty much abandoned in summer.

Since those early days of remodeling we did build a freestanding greenhouse. Our main use is for starting seeds and wintering porch plants. I still long for an attached greenhouse. Someday . . .

Notes for November

December

First Week
STRAWBERRIES

If I had to tell the truth about it, which is almost always desirable, I would say that I really had not planned to spend the first part of a December week putting out strawberry plants when I needed to be doing all manner of other important things. But my Ed had ordered them and they were here. This was one of the many little character-building pastimes he thoughtfully plans to keep me away from beer joints, pool halls, and other such useless activities. I appreciate his concern.

We have strawberries most every year, but like wives and electric irons, they do wear out after awhile and have to be replaced, although as a rule wives produce longer and better than the average strawberry plant or iron.

We planted Earlidawn and Pocahontas. We have had the latter several years and are always pleased with the quality and taste of the berries.

A small strawberry patch is within the gardening possibilities of almost every homeowner. You can steal a place from the flowers, make a spot in the vegetable garden, have a berry barrel, or put a few plants in a window box. If you use the window box, don't plan to make preserves.

The main thing about strawberries is that they are good. They are wonderful fresh, dabbed into a bit of confectioners' sugar, in ice cream and, along with corn, are the favorites in our home freezer. They are also pretty. What cookbook worth buying doesn't have a color picture of a strawberry shortcake? They are also nutritious containing almost as much vitamin C as oranges.

You can start a strawberry patch most any time of the year except when the ground is frozen or in mid-summer. The usual time for planting is in the spring for harvesting the following spring. Fall planting gets a step ahead of the spring schedule, but they still won't bear until the following year. If any blooms do appear next spring, they should be picked off so the plant can put all its energies into making itself strong the first growing year.

Strawberries are easy to grow but do have four requirements: sun; a well-drained location; adequate water, especially during blooming and bearing season; and a slightly acid soil rich in organic matter.

To get the soil right, dig in rotted manure, material from your humus heap, and a complete fertilizer at the rate of 1 pound per 50 square feet. Because this is no small job, try to do it before the plants arrive.

To determine how many plants you need, consider that each plant should produce slightly less than a quart of berries. Usually about 25 plants per family member will be sufficient for eating fresh, preserving, freezing, and sharing.

There are several ways to set out a patch, but the two most often used are the matted row and hills. In the first, the plants are set 18 to 30 inches apart in 3-foot rows. The runners that develop the first spring are allowed to take root about 8 inches apart all around the mother plant. This gives a wide row, and other developing runners are snipped off. If you allow it to get too crowded, the berries will be small in both size and number.

The hill method involves setting plants 12 to 18 inches apart in more narrow rows, removing all runners as they form, depending entirely on the mother plant for fruit production. This takes a little more time, but the plants produce larger, finer berries and will usually last three or four years instead of the two or three years of the matted-row system. It is also true that what starts off as a hill system frequently ends as a matted row after the first year or so.

Before you plant, whether you are taking established runners from your old bed or have purchased new plants, prune the roots to about 3 inches and keep them immersed in water or covered with damp burlap or something so that the roots never dry.

You can poke a trowel into the soil, pull the soil over, insert the plant, and replace the soil, but there is a better way. Make a little hole with a mound of soil in the middle, sort of like planting roses or irises, and set the plant on it, spreading the roots. Partly fill the hole, then water so the water carries the soil all around the roots. Finish filling the hole with soil. The crowns should be at ground level. If you have 25 or 50 plants, you may do it this way. After about 100 plants, you'll start just poking them into the ground.

If you didn't do so earlier, you can fertilize the established bed. After the first crop is harvested two springs from now, cultivate the row well and fertilize, again at the rate of 1 pound per 50 square feet. Use a heavy mulch several inches thick to keep in moisture and keep down weeds. As it decays you'll be improving your soil.

"They" say not to plant a berry patch where tomatoes, eggplant or peppers grew the year before. I don't know why.

Second Week
SOUTHERN MAGNOLIAS

A tree is a splendid thing. Even if it's the kind that in the fall drops leaves that have to be raked by grumbling husbands, discontented wives, and complaining children, the raking is still a small price to pay for a tree.

There are all kinds of trees, but if you have a house site or a lot of any size at all, you really should have a sweet magnolia at your door.

One listing gives more than 40 varieties of magnolias including those native to our North American continent and the Japanese and Chinese varieties plus all the hybrids they have produced. There is no reason not to expect that almost all of these could live in the Piedmont. They have varying colors of flowers, heights, leaf shapes and other differences but they are

187

all magnolias, unfamiliar though they may be. Many, even most of these, are not readily available to the home gardener because nurseries tend to stock and propagate the better known hence better selling plants.

The one we usually think of when someone says "magnolia" is the southern, or *Magnolia grandiflora,* that magnificent broadleaf evergreen that soars to 70 to 100 feet, presenting us with huge 10-inch blossoms in May and beautiful red seed pods in late summer.

Everybody instantly recognizes the distinctive scent of magnolia, and although it is short lived in the house where the blooms quickly turn brown, the few days it is there are worth the effort of trying to get a bloom.

Because of its large growth habits, the southern magnolia should be treated as a specimen plant set apart so that it has plenty of growing space and isn't squeezed up against other trees.

There are two main ways of propagating the magnolia. The first is by planting the seed that has been soaked until the outer covering comes off. Plant it about ½ inch deep, keep it watered, and wait.

The second method is layering. If you have a tree or your neighbor will let you have a branch, follow this procedure. Select a low branch with old wood, score it on the bottom, but don't cut it all the way through. Put some rooting compound on the cut part to help it along. Scoop out a place in the ground and fill it with a mixture of peat moss and good garden soil. Bend the branch down into this prepared spot and cover it with more of the same soil mixture, then put a brick on top so it won't pop out of the soil again. Leave the tip of the branch out of the ground. It will be the top of your new plant.

Start this in summer or early fall, and if the following spring it has established roots, cut it from its mother tree, but don't dig it up. Let it stay another year, and the second spring dig it with a big ball of earth and reset it in your garden.

Magnolias require an acid soil, so mulch it with rotted manure. This layering business may seem to take forever, but it doesn't really. You can buy bare-root or canned plants that go directly into your yard, but it's sort of fun to root your own.

You can plant broadleaf evergreens in either fall or early spring, but if you are putting out bare-root plants, it's best to do so in the spring so the warm days will get the roots growing right away.

Don't plan to prune your magnolia unless you have to because it is slow to heal. You will probably want to remove the suckers at the base of the tree. Magnolias don't really like to be moved, so don't be surprised if your plant just seems to sit there for a year or two without growing. It isn't dead. It will start growing sometime.

When your magnolia gets some size, you may want to preserve some of the leaves for floral arrangements. With this treatment they are flexible and easy to work with and can be used with either fresh or dried flowers. Water doesn't hurt them. Wash the leaves and crush the stem end. Into a jar pour 1 part glycerine from the drugstore and 2 parts water to a depth of 2 inches. Stand the leaves in this. Replace the water as it is absorbed or evaporates and the mixture will last through several treatments and can be saved. If you are in a great hurry, you can dip the whole leaf in the solution and then stand it in the jar. The leaves will have to stay in the solution about two weeks.

A few of the more common of the other kinds of magnolias are the saucer, star, and sweet bay.

The saucer magnolia, *Magnolia soulangeana,* blooms early in the spring about April and May with white to purple-pink blooms that start off as tall, tightly closed buds that open to flat, saucer-shaped beauties. It will endure light shade but prefers sun. Its maximum height is 30 feet, and it spreads as it grows so that it eventually takes up a right sizable space in your yard, but then not any of the magnolias are petite. This *soulangeana* is a hybrid with many varieties.

189

The star, *Magnolia stellata,* is of Japanese ancestry and puts out its white blooms in spring before the leaves emerge. The petals are more numerous but more narrow than the saucer plant. It is a smaller, wider-growing plant growing to about 15 feet. There is a similar variety, *Magnolia stellata rosea,* sometimes called pink star magnolia which has 4-inch flowers that begin as pink and fade to white.

Another kind which grows as far north as middle Pennsylvania is sweet bay, *Magnolia virginiana.* It has creamy white flowers in June similar to our lovely southern *grandiflora* and grows to 30 feet.

Third Week
CHRISTMAS GREENERY

Decorate your home with real, live, honest-to-goodness evergreens this Christmas. For those people living in large cities who have to sell one of the children to pay the dear prices for evergreens, artificial wreaths are understandable. But for us so near the woodlands and fields and whose yards are filled with boxwood, pine, hemlock, cedar, and hollies of all kinds, live greenery should be the only thing.

There are many kinds available, and pine is a favorite not only because of availability and freshness, but because of the marvelous Christmasy fragrance it gives a room. And if you should have a fire going with poplar wood that snaps and crackles, well, it's almost too wonderful to bear.

Cedar, too, is available and often used for wreaths, garlands, and arrangements. You might get the children to help you with these. There's no reason why you should be the only one in the family with pricked fingers.

Using greenery can be as involved as constructing elaborate wreaths, festoons, and garlands, or as simple as laying a few branches on the mantel. The greenery can be used alone or combined with Christmas ornaments, ribbon, pine cones, tiny toys, candles, angels, or almost any of the traditional Christmas items.

A point to remember in decorating for Christmas is to have one major interest center in the room. A fireplace and mantel, if you are fortunate enough to have these, are almost always that interest. If not, the focal point may be a table or chest top, a wall hanging or a garland with only one or two other minor decorations in the room. You don't want your home to look like a craft shop. Don't feel that every horizontal surface has to be covered with tinsel and pine.

The garland is one of the favorite decorations fashioned from greenery. Its uses are many. It can be draped about mirrors, over a stair, from a mantel, around doorways, and wound about a mail-box post. To make the garland you must have a flexible base so it will drape easily. You can use a strong rope or a small, lightweight brass or nickelplated chain. An advantage of the little chain is that the links give you good wiring places.

Cut the green branches of boxwood, round-leaf holly, cedar, pine, or whatever you're using in short pieces about 5 to 6 inches, tie in little bunches, then wire these little bunches to the chain. Wire them all around the chain, overlapping each time and having all the stems in one direction. If you're doing a long garland for a stair rail or doorway, you'll need quite a large amount of greenery, a large supply of wire, wire cutter, time, and patience. While you're working it is the wise child who does not select this time to ask if she may have twelve girls to spend the night next Saturday.

If you plan to use about the same decorations each year, it is wise to put up a tiny cup hook to support your wreath and leave it there all year rather than to drive a new nail each Christmas. It will hardly be noticed, and if it is, it will be of no matter.

To make a festoon, the large arrangement that looks like a swag, get your clever son or your neighbor's to cut a form from lightweight plywood and cover it with wire mesh from the hardware store. Into this you can stick your greenery and wire your pine cones, nuts, or bright artificial fruit. To eliminate wiring and stapling the cones, nuts, etc., use that marvelous little boon to crafters, the glue gun. The little glue gun was surely made for Christmas, but take seriously the warning to use with care. The hot glue can make a painful burn but used carefully the glue gun is a great helper and timesaver.

With new ribbons and greenery the form will serve you many years. In covering it always put the greenery close together and extend it over the edges so the form doesn't show. You can also staple magnolia leaves onto this form using the center for fruit and nuts.

If making garlands, wreaths, and festoons isn't your cup of tea, do at least stick a few branches of pine in a vase by the fireplace or doorway and put a few sprigs of holly in a bowl on the table.

Holly is considered the good luck tree. The red berries represent Christ's blood and the sharp pins on the leaves his crown of thorns. The old English tradition is that bringing holly into the house is an invitation to the Christ Child to enter.

Foil and tinsel, plastic and electricity are all combined to make home, offices, and stores more beautiful at Christmas time, but for the gardener Christmas means live greenery, pine cones, fruits and nuts all filling his home with freshness, fragrance, and cheer.

Fourth Week
CHRISTMAS CHERRIES

If you're going around making promises to anybody who will listen that next year you're going to start earlier, one thing you can do this afternoon for the next Yuletide is to order the seed for a Christmas cherry. It takes a whole year.

Christmas cherries are really outdoor plants, but in our climate they must be brought inside or they'll be killed. Don't try to keep them indoors year around, though, because they need fresh air and sunshine just like people.

Loved because of its bright red and yellow "cherries" and its dark-green, rich foliage, the Christmas cherry has a lot of aliases. The botanist knows it as *Solanum pseudo-capsicum*, but the home gardener may call it Christmas cherry, Jerusalem cherry, winter cherry, or Cleveland cherry. It's purely a decorative plant, so don't try to make a pie from the fruit.

Although there is one variety, *S. cornuliculum*, which produces 2-foot-high plants, the average plant is about 12 inches and sprinkled with bright berries that range in size from ½ inch to 1 inch in diameter depending on the variety. There are newer varieties including *Solanum capsicastrum* which should be treated as an annual. It grows to 12 inches.

The best way to get a Christmas cherry is to have somebody give you one. Lacking that, you can take stem cuttings or plant seeds. The plants have to be cut back after they fruit, and when the new shoots come out, cut one of these, being sure part of the old plant is included. Put it in a pot filled with sand and set the pot in a box deep enough for you to cover it, plant and all, with a piece of windowpane or other glass. Water the cutting daily and spray the tops. After roots form, transfer the plant to another pot with good soil as with any other pot plant.

If you prefer planting seed, December and January are the times to do it. Plant the seed in a flat and cover with glass. When the little seedlings pop up, remove the glass pane and give the plants plenty of light. As soon as the little plants can be handled, and this can be as early as ½-inch tall, transfer them to a larger pot and keep them in a sunny place, watering well.

In late spring, around May or June, put them outside. You can either set the plants outdoors in the pot or take the plant from the pot and plant it directly into the soil. In summer feed it with liquid fertilizer and give it plenty of water. It should be in the sun. Before frost, put it back in a pot or bring the pot inside, depending on how it was treated earlier.

After they come indoors, the plants need light, water, and air. Don't put them in the path of a draft because it will do them in.

Before Christmas they should have brightly colored "cherries" that you'll enjoy all during the holiday season.

Later, when the leaves begin to drop and the berries shrivel, your plant isn't dead, only tired. Prune it back rather severely. Don't give it any fertilizer during this period and little water. It's in a resting period and you don't want to encourage too much growth. After awhile, when the new shoots start, you can resume watering and add a little houseplant fertilizer. Then in late spring carry it back outside and start all over again.

There are a couple of conditions indoors that the Christmas cherry can't endure. One is heat. They prefer a temperature in the 50s. The other is drafts.

If you want a bushier plant, pinch out the top when it is putting out its new growth in the spring.

If you live in the warmer parts of the Piedmont the Jerusalem cherry will survive as a perennial. The seed-bearing cherries will drop and self-sow and soon you will have a little forest of plants that are almost evergreen.

So start now for next Christmas, or anyway, on your next Christmas cherry.

Notes for December

Partial Listing of Plant Societies in the United States

Compilation is by the American Horticultural Society

African Violet Society of America
P.O. Box 3609
Beaumont, TX 77704
(409) 839-4725

Azalea Society of America, Inc.
P.O. Box 6244
Silver Springs, MD 20901
(301) 593-2415

American Bamboo Society
1101 San Leon Court
Solana Beach, CA 92075
(619) 481-9869

American Begonia Society, Inc.
P.O. Box 1129
Encinitas, CA 92024

American Bonsai Society, Inc.
P.O. Box 358
Keene, NH 03431
(603) 352-9034

American Boxwood Society
P.O. Box 190
Bluemont, VA 22012
(703) 554-8309

The Bromeliad Society
2488 East 49th Street
Tulsa, OK 74105

Cactus and Succulent Society of America, Inc.
P.O. Box 3010
Santa Barbara, CA 93130

American Camellia Society
P.O. Box 1217
Fort Valley, GA 31303
(912) 967-2358

National Chrysanthemum Society, Inc.
2139 Vegas Valley Drive
Las Vegas, NV 89109

American Conifer Society
P.O. Box 242
Severna Park, MD 21146

American Daffodil Society
Route 3, 2302 Byhalia Road
Hernando, MS 38632
(601) 368-6337

American Dahlia Society
14408 Long Avenue
Midlothian, IL 60445
(312) 385-6155

American Fern Society, Inc.
David S. Barrington
Dept. of Botany
University of Vermont
Burlington, VT 05405
(802) 656-3221

Friends of the Fig Society
5715 W. Paul Bryant Drive

Crystal River, FL 32629
(904) 795-0489

American Fuchsia Society
Hall of Flowers
Golden Gate Park
San Francisco, CA 94122
(415) 527-5889

Gardenia Society of America
P.O. Box 879
Atwater, CA 95301
(209) 358-2231

North American Gladiolus Council
9338 Manzanita Drive
Sun City, AZ 85373
(602) 972-4177

American Gourd Society
P.O. Box 274
Mount Gilead, OH 43338
(419) 946-3302

American Hemerocallis Society
1454 Rebel Drive
Jackson, MS 39211
(601) 366-4362

The Herb Society of America
9010 Kirtland-Chardon Road
Mentor, OH 44060
(617) 371-1486

American Hibiscus Society
1615 24th Avenue N.
St. Petersburg, FL 33713

American Hosta Society
3103 Heatherhill
Huntsville, AL 35802
(205) 883-6109

American Iris Society
6518 Beachy Avenue
Wichita, KS 67206
(316) 686-8734

North American Lilac Society
P.O. Box 476
Waukee, IL 50263
(515) 987-1371

American Magnolia Society
907 S. Chestnut Street
Hammond, LA 70403

Marigold Society of America, Inc.
P.O. Box 112
New Britain, PA 18901

International Oleander Society
P.O. Box 3431
Galveston, TX 77552
(409) 765-6294

American Orchid Society, Inc.
6000 S. Olive Avenue
West Palm Beach, FL 33405
(407) 585-8666

American Penstemon Society
P.O. Box 33

Plymouth, VT 05056
(412) 238-4208

American Peony Society
250 Interlachen Road
Hopkins, MN 55343
(612) 938-4706

American Poinsettia Society
P.O. Box 706
Mission, TX 78572
(512) 585-1256

American Rhododendron Society
4885 S. W. Sunrise Lane
Tigard, OR 97224
(503) 620-4038

American Rose Society
P.O. Box 30000
Shreveport, LA 71130
(318) 938-5402

INDEX

INDEX

NOTES

NOTES

Notes

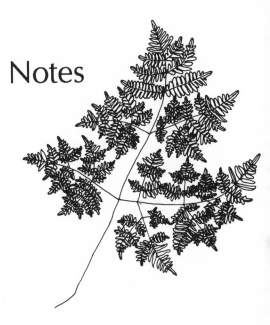